WIT AND WISDOM
OF DEAN INGE

WIT AND WISDOM OF DEAN INGE

SELECTED AND ARRANGED BY
SIR JAMES MARCHANT
K.B.E., LL.D.

WITH A PREFACE BY
WILLIAM RALPH INGE
C.V.O., D.D., F.B.A.: DEAN OF ST. PAUL'S

Essay Index Reprint Series

BOOKS FOR LIBRARIES PRESS
FREEPORT, NEW YORK

First Published 1927
Reprinted 1968

LIBRARY OF CONGRESS CATALOG CARD NUMBER:

68-16941

PRINTED IN THE UNITED STATES OF AMERICA

PREFACE

It is promotion for a writer of books to have a selection from his writings published during his lifetime, and I am grateful to my friend Sir James Marchant for paying me this high compliment. It is, I need not say, Sir James and not myself who asserts that I am witty and wise, or sometimes the one and sometimes the other.

Pereant qui ante nos nostra dixerint. My very first sentence is a reminiscence of Benjamin Whichcote, and an industrious critic may trace some other sayings of mine to an earlier source. Originality, I fear, is too often only undetected and frequently unconscious plagiarism. 'What hast thou that thou didst not receive?'

The extracts are spread over nearly thirty years. Have I altered any of my opinions since I began to write? I have cut out two passages, but I shall not reveal what they are. The rest of my earlier indiscretions have been allowed to stand. I might have expressed some of them rather differently at the present time, but only to make a slight change of emphasis.

I add to my Preface a few gleanings on the subjects touched on in this little book. They will at any rate raise the level of the wit and wisdom which the title may tempt some to look for between its covers.

Preface

Religion.

' Men will never utterly give over the other world for this, nor this world for the other.' (Samuel Butler, the elder.)

' The *reductio ad absurdum* is God's favourite argument.' (George Tyrrell.)

' The fool shall not enter into heaven be he ever so holy.' (William Blake.)

' Religion is too pure for corporations ; it is best meditated on in our privacy, and best acted on in our ordinary inter-course with mankind.' (Landor.)

' A Principal of —— cried out to his assembled pupils, Be Christians and you will be *successful*.' (Santayana.)

' Ce sont les nuances qui se querellent, non les couleurs.' (Tocqueville.)

' God said, Let there be light, and there was light. O thank you, Sir, said the Owl and the Bat ; then we' re off.' (Quiller-Couch.)

' The Reformation that has been. is Luther's monument ; perhaps the Reformation that is to be will trace itself back to Erasmus.' (Beard.)

' The happy man is he that knows the world and cares not for it.' (Joseph Hall, 1574–1656.)

For the Bishop's Study Fireplace. ' Peter stood and warmed himself.'

Disendowment. ' Duc nigras pecudes ; ea prima piacula sunto.' (Virgil.)

Progress.

' The future not being born, my friend, we will abstain from baptizing it.' (Meredith.)

vi

Preface

' L'avenir est un lieu commode pour y mettre les songes.'
(Anatole France.)

' Experience is a good school, but the fees are high.'
(Heine.)

' Ce qui a vraiment vécu une fois revivra.' (Paul Sabatier.)

Democracy.

' Declarations of Independence make nobody really
independent.' (Santayana.)

' The path of freedom is blocked much more by those who
wish to obey than by those who desire to command.'
(M. D. Petre.)

' Thou art a blessed fellow to think as every man thinks ;
never a man's thought in the world keeps the roadway
better than thine.' (Shakespeare.)

' James Mill's creed proceeded less from love to the many
than from hatred to the few.' (Bentham.)

' The public, like Narcissus, is sleepily enamoured of
itself, and the name of its only other perfect lover is Echo.'
(Sir Walter Raleigh, the younger.)

' Government presents only one problem, the discovery of
a trustworthy anthropometric method.' (Bernard Shaw.)

War.

To Herr Krupp. ' Der Reich Gottes ist nicht *Essen*,
sondern . . . Friede.'

' We are glad to have God on our side to maul our
enemies, when we cannot do the work ourselves.' (Dryden.)

' The Army—in times of peace, what ho ! all right !
But in times of war, damnably dangerous department.'
(The Baboo.)

vii

Preface

Literature.

' Le canon a tué la féodalité ; l'encre tuera la société moderne.' (Napoleon.)

' Were angels to write, I fancy we should have but few folios.' (Norris of Bemerton.)

' Hobbes was wont to say that if he had read as much as other men, he should have known no more than other men.' (Aubrey.)

England.

' Englishmen keep in touch with their centre of gravity by rolling heavily from one side to the other.' (Havelock Ellis.)

' Simonides (a foreign statesman) answered one who said to him, " Why is it that the Thessalians (the English) are the only people whom you cannot deceive ? " " They are too stupid (said he) to be deceived by me." ' (Plutarch.)

' All empires die of indigestion.' (Napoleon.)

' Voltaire, whatever be intended, never praised us better than when he said that we have a hundred religions.' (G. M. Trevelyan.)

' Les plus honnêtes gens du monde, ce sont les Français qui pensent et les Anglais qui parlent.' (Saint Évremond.)

Reflections.

' Il est rare qu'un homme soit lancé dans la bataille des idées sans bien vite devenir le comédien de ses premières sincérités.' (Bourget.)

' Rien de plus dangereux que la demi-absurdité ; car l'humanité est mediocre ; elle vomit le trop fort virus ; elle

viii

Preface

vivote avec la dose de sottise qui n'est pas suffisante pour la tuer.' (?)

'Half our mistakes in life arise from feeling where we ought to think, and thinking where we ought to feel.' (Churton Collins.)

> ' Joy and woe are woven fine,
>   A clothing for the soul divine.
>   Under every grief and pine
>   Runs a joy with silken twine.
>   It is right it should be so ;
>   Man was made for joy and woe ;
>   And when this we rightly know
>   Safely through the world we go.'   (William Blake.)

For Page 27.

' Experta vitae consitum spinis iter
    Clausit tenellum lumen et vidit Deum.'   (Quoted in
    Lodge's ' Christopher.')

W. R. INGE.

NOTE

The Publishers are indebted to the following firms for their kindness in giving permission for the inclusion in this volume of quotations from works published by them, viz., for quotations from England, Messrs. Ernest Benn, Ltd., and Messrs. Charles Scribner's Sons; from the Bampton Lectures on Christian Mysticism, Messrs. Methuen & Co., Ltd., and Messrs. Charles Scribner's Sons; from Cambridge Essays in Education, edited by A. C. Benson, the Cambridge University Press; from Lay Thoughts of a Dean, Messrs. G. P. Putnam's Sons, Ltd.

CONTENTS

PART I

RELIGION

Contents

WIT AND WISDOM OF DEAN INGE

PART I

RELIGION

1 RELIGION OF THE SPIRIT

WE cannot make a religion for others, and we ought not to let others make a religion for us. Our own religion is what life has taught us. If we can clarify this body of experience, which comes to us so turbid and impure, we shall have done what is best worth doing for ourselves, and we shall have to offer to others the best that was in us to give, however small its value may be.

2 The true religion for each of us is the most spiritual view of reality that we are able to realise and live by. The forms are not and cannot be the same for all; and accusations of infidelity on the one side, and of obscurantism on the other, are out of place.

3 The spiritual life is a grand experiment which ends in an experience; but it is not merely a leap in the dark; throughout its whole course there is a progres-

sive verification of its fundamental hypothesis, which
makes us quite sure that we are on the right road.
It is much like climbing a mountain. We are too
much occupied with finding our way and securing
footholds to think much about the elevation which
we have reached; but from time to time we observe
that we are nearer the summit, by the larger prospect
which has opened around us. For the fuller revelation we look forward. Our world is still in the making, and we are in the making too. We look to the
Christus futurus to interpret the Christ of past history,
and to the *homo futurus* to show us what is the meaning
of human personality.

4 The religion of the Spirit, that autonomous faith
which rests upon experience and individual inspiration, has seldom had much of a chance in the world
since the Christian revelation, in which it received
its full and final credentials. We may call it the
Platonic tradition, since the school of Plato ended by
being completely dominant in the last age of classical
antiquity. We may venture to call it the true heir
of the original Gospel, while admitting that no direct
Hellenic influence can be traced in our Lord's teaching. We may confidently call it Pauline and Johannine Christianity, though the theology of St. Paul
is woven of many strands. We find it explicitly
formulated by Clement and Origen, and we may
appeal to one side of that strangely divided genius,
Augustine. It lives on in the mystics, especially in
the German mediaeval school, of which Eckhart is

the greatest name. We find it again, with a new
and exuberant life, in many of the Renaissance writers.
Our own Renaissance poetry is steeped in Platonic
thoughts. Later, during the civil troubles of the
seventeenth century, it appears in a very pure and
attractive form in the little group of Cambridge
Platonists, Whichcote, Smith, Cudworth, and their
friends. In the unmystical eighteenth century Jacob
Böhme takes captive the manly and robust intellect
of William Law, and inspires him to write some of
the finest religious treatises in the English language.
Meanwhile, the Quakers had the root of the matter
in them, but they have only recently discovered their
spiritual affinities with Plato. The tradition has never
been extinct; or we may say more truly that the fire
which, in the words of Eunapius, ' still burns on the
altars of Plotinus,' has a perennial power of rekindling
itself when the conditions are favourable. But the
repressive forces of tyranny and bigotry have prevented
the religion of the Spirit from bearing its proper
fruits. The luck of history, we may say, has hitherto
been unfavourable to what I, at least, hold to be the
growth of the divine seed. It has either fallen on the
rock or by the wayside, or the thorns have grown up
with it and choked it. The religion of the Spirit
has an intrinsic survival value, which is quite different
from the extrinsic survival value of the religion of
authority. Authority may for a time diminish the
number of dissentients by burning their bodies or
their books; but ' On ne tue pas des idées par coup
de baton.'

5 MYSTICISM

I think we may enumerate the characteristics of mystical religion as follows. (1) It is a disinterested quest of the absolutely real and good and beautiful. It is disinterested : the quest is for its own sake, never for anything outside itself. ' If a man will seek the Good for anything beyond itself, he will never find it.' And it is a quest of the Absolute. The mystic's goal is God Himself—the unchanging, eternal fountain of all being, the summit of all reality. There is no relativity in the mystic's philosophy, when we reach the end of it. His values are absolute ; he desires and hopes to reach the bare truth, the unconditional good, the beauty which Plato describes and contrasts with the visible beauties which we know on earth. (2) The mystic stakes all to gain all ; he gives his whole self, because if anything is kept back the quest is vain. As Manilius says :—

Quid caelo dabimus ? Quantum est, quo veneat omne ?
Impendendus homo est, Deus esse ut possit in ipso.

Huxley once said : ' It does not take much of a man to be a Christian, but it takes all there is of him.' (3) He is committed to a life of strenuous labour, though the labour is mostly internal. The prize can be won only at the price of lifelong struggle. (4) Although the journey is through darkness to light, and although, as Isaac Pennington says, ' All truth is shadow except the last,' yet there is *immediacy* all through. Something within us is in contact with the

4

Divine; there is a 'spark' at the core of the soul which was kindled at the altar in heaven, and which even sin cannot quite extinguish. (5) The goal is a living object of love, a God who draws souls like a magnet. (6) Beatitude is a form of enriched and enhanced life, not nothingness, whatever some mystics may say about entering into the silence, and being free from life's vain shadows. Not *nirvana*, but peace bathed in love, is his aim; and his path is a dying life, not a living death.

6   Mysticism is a spiritual philosophy which demands the concurrent activity of thought, will, and feeling. It assumes from the outset that these three elements of our personality, which in real life are never sundered from each other, point towards the same goal, and if rightly used will conduct us thither. Further, it holds that only by the consecration of these three faculties in the service of the same quest can a man become effectively what he is potentially, a partaker of the Divine nature and a denizen of the spiritual world. There is no special organ for the reception of Divine or spiritual truth, which is simply the knowledge of the world as it really is. Some are better endowed with spiritual gifts than others, and are called to ascend greater heights; but the power which leads us up the pathway to reality and blessedness is, as Plotinus says, one which all possess, though few use it.

7   Even the severest political economist must admit that, if the mystic produces no marketable commo-

dities, he consumes very little of them ; and a more reasonable estimate of human costs and values will lead us to think that no labour is better expended than that which explores the way to the treasure-houses of the spirit, and shows mankind where to find those goods which are increased by being shared, and which none can take from us.

8   Psychology cannot do justice to mysticism because the validity of the mystic's faith lies outside its province, and the methods of psychology almost require it to assume that it has no validity, apart from its purely subjective interest to the devotee's own mind. The psychology of the mystical experience may be and is very interesting to the student of mental science. To the mystic himself his experiences are of no interest or value whatever, except as visions of objective reality not created by his own imagination. He may be right or he may be wrong in believing that he has a glimpse of the world beyond the veil; my point is that the psychologist is almost bound to assume that he is wrong. The admission of real inspiration from above would oblige him to admit into his science a whole range of values which he has excluded from consideration ; it would destroy his hope of bringing all mental states under a closed system.

9   We cannot determine the proper place of the mystical experience, because it is no fixed, self-identical thing. It is an 'untravelled world, whose margin fades for ever and for ever as we move.' As

that which was once in a luminous haze comes into clear daylight, a fresh vision of cloud-capped towers and gorgeous palaces floats dimly into view. There is no rest, no sitting still, no time for voluptuous dreaming, in the spiritual journey, until we reach the land which is still very far off, though it lies all about us and within us, closer than breathing and nearer than hands and feet. We do not ask to see the distant scene; we know that we must climb by degrees. 'Beloved, now are we the sons of God; and it doth not yet appear what we shall be; but we know that when He shall be manifested, we shall be like Him, for we shall see Him as He is.' The last words express the fundamental faith of all mystics, that like is known by like, and only by like. 'We could not see the sun'—so they tell us in an illustration which is a favourite with them—'if we had not something sun-like in our eyes.'

10 The practice of the presence of God may involve very many hours of hard work; but the reward is great; for this is the joy that no man can take from us; this is the faith which is the human side of divine grace, an experiment which is becoming an experience, a foretaste and assurance of the rest that remaineth for the people of God.

11 There is, therefore, no substitute for first-hand experience in the spiritual life. We must believe the explorers of the high places of the unseen world when they tell us that they have been there, and found what

they sought. But they cannot really tell us *what* they found ; if we wish to see what they have seen, we must live as they have lived.

12   At the core of our personality is a spark lighted at the altar of God in heaven—a something too holy ever to consent to evil, an inner light which can illuminate our whole being. To purify the eyes of the understanding by constant discipline, to detach ourselves from hampering worldly or fleshly desires, to accustom ourselves to ascend in heart and mind to the kingdom of the eternal values which are the thoughts and purposes of God—this is the quest of the mystic and the scheme of his progress through his earthly life. It carries with it its own proof and justification, in the increasing clearness and certainty with which the truths of the invisible world are revealed to him who diligently seeks for them. The experience is too intimate, and in a sense too formless, to be imparted to others. Language was not made to express it, and the imagination which recalls the hours of vision after they have passed paints the vision in colours not its own. Remembered revelation always tends to clothe itself in mythical or symbolic form. But the revelation was real; and it is here, and here only—in the mystical act *par excellence*, the act of prayer—that faith passes for a time into sight. Formless and vague and fleeting as it is, the mystical experience is the bed-rock of religious faith. In it the soul, acting as a unity with all its faculties, rises above itself and becomes spirit ; it asserts its claim to be a citizen of heaven.

13 I am very far from claiming that I have had these rich experiences myself. It is only occasionally that I can ' pray with the spirit and pray with the understanding also,' a very different thing from merely ' saying one's prayers.' Nor have I found in the contemplation of nature anything like the inspiration which Wordsworth and others have described. At times ' the moving waters at their priest-like task ' seem to have the power which Euripides ascribes to them, of ' washing away all human ills ' ; at times the mountains speak plainly of the Ancient of Days who was before they began to be ; but too often nature only echoes back my own moods, and seems dark or bright because I am sad or merry. The sweet sanctities of home life, and especially the innocence and affection of young children, more often bring me near to the felt presence of God. But for the testimony of the great cloud of witnesses, who have mounted higher and seen more, I should not have ventured to build so much on this immediate revelation of God to the human soul. But the evidence of the saints seems to me absolutely trustworthy ; and the dimness of my own vision would be disquieting only if I felt that I had deserved better. The pearl of great price is not so easily found. But do we know of any who have sought after the knowledge of God as diligently as other men seek after wealth and honour, and have come away empty-handed ?

14 It is not claimed that Mysticism, even in its widest sense, is, or can ever be, the whole of Christianity.

Every religion must have an institutional as well as a mystical element. Just as, if the feeling of immediate communion with God has faded, we shall have a dead Church worshipping 'a dead Christ,' as Fox the Quaker said of the Anglican Church in his day, so, if the seer and prophet expel the priest, there will be no discipline and no cohesion. Still, at the present time, the greatest need seems to be that we should return to the fundamentals of spiritual religion. We cannot shut our eyes to the fact that both the old seats of authority, the infallible Church and the infallible book, are fiercely assailed, and that our faith needs reinforcements. These can only come from the depths of the religious consciousness itself; and if summoned from thence, they will not be found wanting. The 'impregnable rock' is neither an institution nor a book, but a life or experience. Faith, which is an affirmation of the basal personality, is its own evidence and justification. Under normal conditions, it will always be strongest in the healthiest minds. There is and can be no appeal from it. If, then, our hearts, duly prepared for the reception of the Divine Guest, at length say to us, ' This I know, that whereas I was blind, now I see,' we may, in St. John's words, ' have confidence towards God.'

15 GOD

The Godhead as He is in Himself, all great mystics have agreed, is indescribable and unimaginable; no names can be given Him and no statements made about Him. Even the Trinity, some have thought, must proceed from a mysterious Unity 'beyond existence.' But this does not mean that we ought to abstain from attributing any qualities to God. To do this would be to impoverish our religion, not to bring it closer to the truth. The organ by which we know God is our whole personality unified under the primacy of the highest part of it. God for us is the best that we can know. The spirit of man is not confined by time and place; but it is *ensouled* spirit, the spirit-in-soul of a being under probation in a world of time and place. Our highest intuitions of the Divine, our most intimate communications with God, must still be relative to the condition in which we are; and if, following the path of logic and analysis, we strip off those determinations which genuine religious experience attaches to the idea of God, we shall be in danger of defaecating to a transparency what ought to be the most richly concrete idea in our consciousness. St. Paul, in that inspired hymn which proclaims Love to be the hierophant of the Divine mysteries, ends by emphasising the necessary limitations of our knowledge. 'Now we see as in a mirror, by symbols, but then face to face; now I know in part, but then shall I know even as I am known.' The apostle's 'now' and 'then' are themselves symbolic, being derived from the lower categories of experience, like the 'here' and 'there' of the Platonist.

16   God has spoken to us all, once or twice or more often, as a man speaketh unto his friend. There have

been moments in the lives of each one of us, in which the spirit's true endowments stand out plainly from its false ones, and apprise it if pursuing or the right way or the wrong way, to its triumph or undoing. We must ' cherish these best hours of the mind,' as Bacon says, and not let them slip from us. We shall find them very helpful in moments of doubt and despondency.

17   Much time is not required for the practice of the presence of God, after that practice has once become a habit. The habit once formed, our work, however exacting, will help rather than hinder ; it will bring fuel to the fire upon the altar.

18   So the whole of religion is summed up in the vision of God. . . . Our struggle to reach Him is at the same time a struggle for self-liberation. We lose our Soul in order to find it again in God. There is no barrier between the human and Divine natures. The human Soul has only to strip itself of those outer integuments which are no part of its true nature, in order to expand freely by means of the ' organic filaments ' which unite it with all spiritual being.

19 THE INCARNATION
    The Incarnation is a proclamation that ' the All-great is the All-loving too '—a doctrine which few, I think, accept who do not believe in the Incarnation of the Son of God in Christ. And if, with the

Church of the Creeds and Fathers, we accept something like the Logos-doctrine already held by St. Paul and briefly summarised by St. John, we have the most inspiring thought that the laws of the universe, in their deepest meaning, are the expression of the character of the creating and sustaining Word who became flesh and tabernacled among us in the person of Jesus of Nazareth. I need not dwell on the consecration of the whole of nature which follows from this belief; on the final repudiation of that unfortunate dualism between the natural and supernatural which has introduced chaos into both spheres, natural and spiritual alike; on the sanction which it gives to the pursuits of poetry, art, and science, as being each, in their different ways, a priestly and prophetic office, revealing to us the God whom we know in our hearts as the Good, under His other attributes of the True and the Beautiful. The world is good, for God the Word made it; but it can be made better, for He came to redeem it. And His redeeming, transforming work did not come to an end when He left the earth; we are living under the dispensation which then began, a dispensation of progressive enlightenment and steady realisation of a great purpose—the achievement of a theophany in redeemed humanity itself.

20   That the Incarnation should have taken the form of a human life lived under ordinary conditions causes me no difficulty. A perfect human character, with human limitations, is the only possible form of an Incarnation for the benefit of mankind. Nothing

would have been added, and much would have been lost if the Incarnate had been invested with the trappings of earthly power, or with superhuman majesty and beauty of person. Still less, in my opinion, ought we to demand that He should break through the fixed laws of nature, which He Himself ordained, and in accordance with which He orders the course of the world. In so doing He would not have exalted Himself; He would have condemned His own creation.

21 There is another consideration which makes the orthodox Christology precious to me. It illustrates the extreme patience with which God works. The divine in humanity is, it appears, a leaven which very slowly transforms the whole lump, and is not less divine because it operates very slowly. The Incarnation, though in one sense it came in the fullness of time, was in another sense very premature. Not only was Christ rejected by the large majority of His own contemporaries, but His message was soon so swallowed in the three measures of meal that it was to all appearance almost lost.

22 It is not . . . in the Gospels only that we are to look for the record of the Incarnation and for its fruits. The Church was meant to be the depository of the divine indwelling; and though the public policy of the Church may seem to display few signs of divine guidance, the lives of the saints do not disappoint us. The Christ whom the Church has worshipped is a

fuller and richer revelation of the Son of God than the Jesus whom the Evangelists have depicted. There is no necessity for drawing contrasts between the Christ of history and the Christ of faith, as if faith and fact could possibly be independent of each other. We are not driven to acknowledging *comme deux Christs* with Loisy. The Christ of the Church is the same Christ as Jesus of Nazareth; but the Church understands who and what He is more fully than those could who walked with Him on the shores of Gennesaret. It was expedient for us that He should go away.

23 THE CROSS

. . . The great message of the *Cross* stands or falls with the divinity of Christ. Is it not the truth that all the rivals of Christianity fail just here? All the religious philosophies of antiquity, it seems to me, shrink, in the last resort, from grasping the nettle of suffering quite firmly. They all want to make us invulnerable, somehow. There must always be a back-door of escape if the ills of life become too over-powering. Either defiant resistance, or suicide, or complete detachment, is recommended. By some means or other, the man himself must be rescued from circumstance, he must provide himself with a magic impenetrable armour. And *therefore*, the sting of pain is never drawn. The good news of Christianity is that suffering is itself divine. It is not foreign to the experience of God Himself. ' In all their afflic-tion He was afflicted.' ' Surely He hath borne our

griefs and carried our sorrows.' ' If thou be the
Son of God,' said His enemies, ' come down from the
Cross.' No : not while any man remains unredeemed.
The divine suffering is not an episode, but a revelation.
It is the necessary form which divine love takes, when
it is brought into contact with evil. To overcome
evil with good means to suffer unjustly and willingly.

24　It is the blasphemy of ' Christian Science ' and
kindred movements to deny the Cross. And in our
soft, self-indulgent age it is, shamefully, felt to be
a greater difficulty in the way of belief in God that
men should suffer than that men should sin. This
timid, pain-dreading temper is thoroughly unchristian.
It is still unchristian when, as often happens to good
people nowadays, they are idealists in their devotions
and in their philosophy, but materialists in their
charities and their politics. I believe that one reason
of this is that we imagine other people's sufferings to
be greater than they are, and so we are able to bear
our own misfortunes with more faith and courage
than those of our friends, or those of the very poor,
who are often only too happy in their reckless enjoyment of each day as it comes. This temper necessarily
leads to pessimism, since no amount of protestation
that ' it doesn't hurt,' and no amount of philanthropy,
can remove the stubborn fact that pain and sorrow
and disappointment are bound up with the other
laws of human life, and that we must bear them,
whether we like it or not. ' Ducunt volentem fata,
nolentem trahunt.'

25 HOLY COMMUNION

The Holy Communion is the Sacrament in and by which we are to remember Him, and in remembering to be united to Him. The culmination of the life of prayer is the reception of the life of God within us, and this is the mystery of the Eucharist. Whether or not it be true, as the mystics of all ages have taught, that there is a ' soul-centre ' which is as it were the natural point of contact with the Divine, an unquenchable spark from the altar in heaven, a principle which does not and cannot consent to sin, and which, as William Law says, ' is so infinite that nothing can satisfy it, or give it any rest, but the infinity of God,' at any rate in this sacrament the ' medicine of immortality' is offered us, and offered in the name and through the mediation of Jesus Christ. ' Whoso eateth my flesh and drinketh my blood hath eternal life.'

26   The two great sacraments are typical symbols, if we use the word in the sense which I give to it, as something which, in being what it is, is a sign and vehicle of something higher and better. This is what the early Church meant when it called the sacraments symbols. A ' symbol' at that period implied a mystery, and a ' mystery ' implied a revelation. The need of sacraments is one of the deepest convictions of the religious consciousness. It rests ultimately on the instinctive reluctance to allow any spiritual fact to remain without an external expression. It is obvious that all morality depends on the application of this principle to conduct. All voluntary external acts are symbolic of (that is,

17   c

vitally connected with) internal states, and cannot be divested of this their essential character. It may be impossible to show how an act of the material body can purify or defile the immaterial spirit; but the correspondence between the outward and inward life cannot be denied without divesting morality of all meaning. . . . Every act of the will is the expression of a state of the soul; and every state of the soul must seek to find expression in an act of the will. Love, as we should all admit, is not love, so long as it is content to be only in thought, or 'in word and in tongue'; it is only when it is love 'in deed' that it is love 'in truth.' And it is the same with all other virtues, which are in this sense symbolic, as implying something beyond the external act. Nearly all the states or motions of the soul can find their appropriate expression in action. Charity in its manifold forms need not seek long for an object; and thankfulness and penitence, though they drive us first to silent prayer, are not satisfied till they have borne fruit in some act of gratitude or humility. But that deepest sense of communion with God, which is the very heart of religion, is in danger of being shut up in thought and word, which are inadequate expressions of any spiritual state. No doubt this highest state of the soul may find indirect expression in good works; but these fail to express the *immediacy* of the communion which the soul has felt. The want of symbols to express these highest states of the soul is supplied by sacraments.

27   When we receive the Holy Communion, we express our belief that the mysterious Divine presence, of

which we are conscious in prayer (using, once more, the word 'prayer' of all communings of the soul with the unseen spiritual world)—that this mysterious Divine presence is not only God, or the spirit of God, but 'the Spirit of *Jesus*,' to use a phrase which the Revised Version has restored to our New Testament. We are identifying the living well-spring of our faith, the source of our hope and our happiness, the guide and inspirer of our lives, with a historical character who lived nearly two thousand years ago.

28 INFLUENCE OF CHRIST

The twentieth century should know more of Christ than the first. In looking back at the history of Christian thought, how strange have been the garments in which that sacred figure has successively been draped! Every age, every nation has shown a pathetic eagerness to trace in Him the lineaments of its own ideal. Have we not seen Him depicted as an ascetic, as a warrior, as a high-priest, and more recently as *le bon sans-culotte*—as a socialist? Is it disrespectful to say that the Christ of Renan is a Frenchman, the Christ of Seeley's *Ecce Homo* an Englishman, the Christ of some recent German biographies a German of the new type? There is a true instinct behind these naïve distortions of a historical figure. Christ is the universal man, the ideal of humanity; and it is right that He should be 'crowned with many crowns,' as each nation and each century invests Him with its own ideal attributes.

29   Christ never expected, or taught His disciples to
expect, that His teaching would meet wide accept-
ance or exercise political influence. ' The world '—
organised human society—was the enemy, and was
to continue the enemy. His message, He foresaw,
would be scorned and rejected by the majority ; and
those who preached it were to expect persecution.
This warning is repeated so often in the Gospels that
it would be superfluous to give quotations. He made
it quite plain that the big battalions are never likely
to be gathered before the narrow gate. He declared
that only false prophets are well spoken of by the
majority. When we consider the revolutionary
character of the Christian idealism, its indifference to
nearly all that passes for ' religion ' with the vulgar,
and its reversal of all current valuations, it is plain
that it is never likely to be a popular creed. As
surely as the presence of high spiritual instincts in
the human mind guarantees its indestructibility, so
surely the deeply rooted prejudices which keep the
majority on a lower level must prevent the Gospel
of Christ from dominating mundane politics or social
life.

30   Moreover, the actual extent of the Gospel's influence cannot be estimated. The inwardness and
individualism of its teaching make its apparent
effectiveness smaller than its real power, which works
secretly and unobserved. The vices which Christ
regarded with abhorrence are perversions of character
—hypocrisy, hard-heartedness, and worldliness or

secularity; and who can say what degree of success the Gospel has achieved in combating these? The method of Christianity is alien to all externalism and machinery; it does not lend itself to those accommodations and compromises without which nothing can be done in politics. As Harnack says, the Gospel is not one of social improvement, but of spiritual redemption. Its influence upon social and political life is indirect and obscure, operating through a subtle modification of current valuations, and curbing the competitive and acquisitive instincts, which nearly correspond with what Christ called ' mammon ' and St. Paul ' the flesh.' Christianity is a spiritual dynamic, which has very little to do directly with the mechanism of social life.

31   Real Christianity is a revolutionary idealism, which estranges conservatives because it is revolutionary, and the revolutionary because it is idealistic. At the same time, it sanctions and blesses the purest motives of both sides. It binds together the living present and the living past; it brings out of its treasure things new and old; old things which are ever new, and new things which were in the counsels of God before the world began. It proclaims equality, and counsels submission; it denounces luxury, and preaches contentment. It increases immeasurably the world's stock of those values which the world does not care for.

32   The Christian is to conquer nature only by studying and obeying her. . . . He will use no force, no

fraud, no devil's engines of any kind, to advance His kingdom. He will not even ' forbid ' rival teachers if they teach the truth. Let others scheme, and forge documents, and persecute and flatter the strongest powers in the State—whether the strongest be that ' *vultus instantis tyranni* ' or the ' *civium ardor prava iubentium.*' He will do none of these things. He will wait patiently till the leaven has done its work. And this, if we believe that Christ is God, must be the only method of working for and with God which God approves. He who took a million years to mould a block of old red sandstone is willing to take a good many thousand years to mould humanity into His own likeness. The practical application of this lesson is too obvious to need many words ; it is just this : Play no tricks and cut no knots.

33 ETERNAL LIFE

Eternity is an experience and a conception partly latent and partly patent in all human life. It is in part defined to our consciousness negatively. Of things in place and time we say : This thing is outside that. They cannot coincide or amalgamate ; hence they are different. And again we say, This thing comes after that. The former must disappear before the latter can arrive ; hence they are different. But our minds tell us that there is a large class of things of which these statements are untrue. These things do not interfere with each other or displace each other. They are alive and active, but they are neither born nor die. They are constant without inertia; they are active, but they do not move. Our knowledge of the eternal order is as direct as our knowledge of the temporal order; but our customary habits of thought and modes of speech confuse us. To be honest, we can think most clearly of eternal life when we divest the conception of its ethical associations; but this is to cut the nerve which links the temporal and the eternal. It will lead us to acosmism, for this world will then have no meaning; or, since 'outraged nature has her occasional revenges,' we may swing round into materialism. And the interpenetration of time and eternity in our consciousness, though it may spoil or confound the symmetry of our metaphysics, is, after all, a fact of the soul-nature, in which we live and move. Reason seeks to divide them, assigning to Caesar and to God what belongs to each; but in the true spiritual experience they are not divided. Time is a child of eternity, and 'resembles its parent as much as it can.'

34   The loss of faith in eternal life seems to be the just Nemesis of individualism. It is instructive and rather pathetic to see how some turn to such 'evidence' for survival after death as has been collected by Mr. Frederick Myers. One would have supposed that this kind of immortality—in which we apparently show our continued activity only by occasionally terrifying our surviving friends—would have had no attractions for any one. And one would have supposed that men who have had some experience

of human credulity and self-deception would have disdained to dabble in spiritualism. But the individualist, who has staked everything on his own self-existent personality, who can hardly think of immortality except as survival in time (time being to him absolutely real), and who is puzzled to say how immortality thus conceived can be the destiny of mankind, really needs evidence of this sort; and since no good evidence is forthcoming, he must be content with bad. Many others, as the *questionnaires* lately circulated in America and England have proved, have the courage to say that they do not desire this kind of personal survival in time.

35   A kingdom of heaven inhabited by a population of spiritual monads, the number of which is determined by the fluctuations in the birth-rate and the duration of human life on this planet, or, as Anselm and others believed, by the amount of the accommodation available in heaven after the expulsion of the fallen angels, is hardly credible even as a symbolic picture. If we once realise that dreams of a heaven in which *we* ourselves are the centre are a transference to the eternal world of those selfish schemes and imaginings which are the essence of sin, we should put them away from us, and thereby remove from our path the chief stumbling-block in the way of belief in our eternal destiny. Our personal life has a meaning and a value; that value and that meaning are eternal; there is no danger of their being ever lost. Still less is there any danger of love ever perishing for want of its object. Love is

divine, and implies immortality. Nor should we ever forget that we are deciding by our lives here our rank in the eternal world. But the Christian eschatology, avowedly symbolical as it is, becomes grotesque and incredible symbolism if we transfer to heaven and hell the crude notions of individuality which for the most part pass unchallenged in the West.

36   The feeling of the contrast between what ought to be and what is, is one of the deepest springs of faith in the unseen. It can only be ignored by shutting our eyes to half the facts of life. It is easy to say with Browning, ' God's in His heaven : all's right with the world,' or with Emerson, that justice is not deferred, and that everyone gets exactly his deserts in this life ; but it would require a robust confidence or a hard heart to maintain these propositions while standing among the ruins of an Armenian village, or by the deathbed of innocence betrayed. There is no doubt a sense in which it may be said that the ideal is the actual ; but only when we have risen in thought to a region above the antitheses of past, present, and future, where ' *is* ' denotes, not the moment which passes as we speak, but the everlasting Now in the mind of God. This is not a region in which human thought can live ; and the symbolical eschatology of religion supplies us with forms in which it is possible to think. The basis of the belief in future judgment is that deep conviction of the rationality of the world-order, or, in religious language, of the wisdom and justice of God, which we cannot and will not sur-

render. It is authenticated by an instinctive assurance which is strongest in the strongest minds, and which has nothing to do with any desire for spurious ' consolations ' ; it is a conviction, not merely a hope, and we have every reason to believe that it is part of the Divine element in our nature. This conviction, like other mystical intuitions, is formless : the forms or symbols under which we represent it are the best that we can get. They are, as Plato says, ' a raft ' on which we may navigate strange seas of thought far out of our depth. We may use them freely, as if they were literally true, only remembering their symbolical character when they bring us into conflict with natural science, or when they tempt us to regard the world of experience as something undivine or unreal.

37 Our hearts tell us of a higher form of existence, in which the doom of death is not merely deferred but abolished. This eternal world we here see through a glass darkly : at best we can apprehend but the outskirts of God's ways, and hear a small whisper of His voice ; but our conviction is that, though our earthly house be dissolved (as dissolved it must be), we have a home not made with hands, eternal in the heavens. In this hope we may include all creation ; and trust that in some way neither more nor less incomprehensible than the deliverance which we expect for ourselves, all God's creatures, according to their several capacities, may be set free from the bondage of corruption and participate in the final triumph over death and sin. Most firmly do I believe

that this faith in immortality, though formless and impalpable as the air we breathe, and incapable of definite presentation except under inadequate and self-contradictory symbols, is nevertheless enthroned in the centre of our being, and that those who have steadily set their affections on things above, and lived the risen life even on earth, receive in themselves an assurance which robs death of its sting, and is an earnest of a final victory over the grave.

38 CHRISTIAN SAINTLINESS—I

OUR LITTLE DAUGHTER

Our little daughter, Margaret Paula, . . . entered into her rest on the night of Thursday in Holy Week, 1923. It is not congenial to me to tear aside the veil which secludes the sanctities of a happy home. . . . But it has been my strange privilege, as I believe, to be the father of one of God's saints, a character as pure and beautiful as many which are recorded in the Church's roll of honour ; and I offer these pages which are to follow as a thank-offering for that precious gift, not without hope that my readers may be able, from this slight and meagre record, to realise something of the beauty and fragrance which accompanied that short but not imperfect life of eleven years.

We remember her first as a fine baby with a strong will of her own. But before long she became a fairy child, very graceful in her movements, very gentle and loving, and at times rather dreamy. She was only five

years old when a friend with whom she was staying
wrote : ' Paula has an intense sweetness of disposition,
so heavenly in her sweetness, gentleness and tender-
ness.' This was the impression which she made in-
creasingly on all who knew her, and it was the verdict
of the nursery. On the day of her death I took her
little brother on my knee, and told him that Paula was
going to spend her Easter with Jesus Christ. After a
good cry he said : ' In all her long life—at least it
seems a long life to me, though not to you—Paula has
never made anybody angry ; she has always made
everybody happy.' There was hardly ever any
quarrelling in her presence.

She was taken ill eighteen months before she died,
and during the whole of that time she had to live on
a very low diet, without any of the dainties which
children love. She bore the privation with a serenity
and patience which astonished the doctors and nurses,
who declared that they had never seen such a child.
She continued to speak to us as if she expected to get
well, but I think she really knew as much as we did.
A few months before the end her little brother said to
her when they were alone, ' O Paula, I wish you would
get better.' The little boy was so much impressed by
her answer that he repeated it to his mother. ' No,
Richard, you must not say that. God has spared me
for a whole year to be with you all, and it has been
the happiest year of my life.' A little later, when she
was no longer able to use her pencil and paint-box, she
said to her mother : ' I am the happiest little girl in
all the world.' It seemed to us that this happiness

came from a vivid realisation that the everlasting arms were about her, and from a consciousness that the deep love which she felt for us all, including her kind doctor and nurse, was fully returned.

It was wonderful to see how quickly her character matured under the discipline of weakness. The words, ' She is a real saint,' were often spoken of her, and they seemed to us to be no more than the truth. On Palm Sunday I repeated to her Milton's sonnet on his blindness ; and when I came to ' They also serve who only stand and wait,' I thought it right to say, ' Paula, I should like you to remember that last line. You will never know how much you have done for all of us in this house, and for many others, simply by being what God has helped you to be.' She was much pleased, and asked for the line again and again during the next two days.

Till the very end she was busy with her needle, making Easter presents for her parents, brothers and sister. During the last weeks she asked to discontinue her childlike practice of saying her prayers aloud to her mother or nurse. She said, ' If you do not mind, I should like best to be quite alone with God.'

It was on Tuesday in Holy Week that she said to her nurse : ' Nannie, when Good Friday comes, I want you to take all my flowers and lay them with your own hands on the soldiers' monument at Westminster.' The nurse said : ' But I could not leave you, Paula. One of the maids can take the flowers if you wish to send them.' She replied : ' I can't help being glad that you think you ought not to

leave me ; but I did mean that to be my Good Friday
penance.' The flowers were placed on the Cenotaph,
as she had desired ; but there were no more penances
for her on Good Friday. She had already heard her
Saviour say, 'This day shalt thou be with me in
Paradise.'

The letters—there were nearly a thousand—which
came in after her death, showed how many outside
the family had understood what she was. Her nurse
wrote to Paula's mother : ' I am trying to describe the
beautiful and lovely character of dear little Paula.
Never before have I met with so sweet and brave a
nature. In spite of her illness, her last year has been
wonderful. Being a Fairy Princess (as she really
thought herself) she lived in a sweet imagination, loving
all things beautiful, and doing things as a Princess
should. On her fast days she often said, " I am a
Princess, so I must not feel hungry." Apart from her
fairy imagination, she loved everything that was good
and holy, never forgetting her prayers or Bible and
loving her little hymns, always mindful of that higher
kingdom which was waiting for her. I like to think
of those last few days. It was so wonderful to see
her goodness and patience. Several times she said,
" Nanna, I am so happy " ; although perhaps she did
not know why, but I suppose it was just God's sweet
peace in her heart. I am glad to have been with her
for the last year of her life. She was so pleased to have
a Nanna all to herself.'

The hospital nurse also wrote : ' She was so good
and patient, filling her little corner of the world

with a very wonderful fragrance. No one will forget her.'

The little group of girls who initiated her into their Fairy Land game, and crowned her with a charming ceremony as 'Princess Asphodel,' loved her dearly. They made her a fairy dress for her 'coronation,' and this little scene will live in the memories of all who were present. One of them wrote : ' She was one of the most lovely things I have ever known, and it has been a very wonderful year since I have known her, and the years will continue so, more and more lovely for her sake.' And another : 'What a wonderful fairy story is Paula's this week, beyond anything we could imagine for her. And how truly she is the Princess of the Spring. The daffodils must always be her flowers now ; she looked so like a pale daffodil herself, in that yellow velvet. But all beautiful things belong to Paula, and to know her is something to be thankful for.'

Another, who is captain of an East End company of ' Brownies,' inducted her into that corps, and taught the poor children to honour her as the model Brownie. They came in their little russet uniforms to the funeral, and escorted the coffin as a guard of honour. Afterwards they came again to see her room. The ' Brown Owl ' wrote : ' I have only known Paula since last May, but in that time I learnt to love and admire her more than anyone else I have ever known. I know that at least thirty-eight wee Brownies will truly miss their little friend, who to them (and to others) was a little Princess and an ideal Brownie.'

Two or three other tributes may be quoted as representative of many more. ' I always felt there was something so deeply attractive about Paula, something a little detached, a little mysterious, almost as if she knew something that was hidden from us—some secret too deep for revealing; a little wistful too, as if she would have shared that secret if she could.'

One who was present at the first part of the funeral service, in St. Paul's, says : ' It was quite the most beautiful memorial service I have ever been to. It was all so simple, and yet so much dignity ; so little pomp and yet all so regal, such true feeling and true pathos on every side. One felt the beautiful spirit of that saint-like nature—the loving spirit of Paula—over everything. It was so wonderful, the tribute from the whole of that great city to Paula ; all the traffic stopped, the flowers, the silent tribute from the public, and the great quiet and peace. It was very wonderful.' Another wrote : ' I thought it so impressive to see that silent mass of bareheaded City men paying respect to that sweet frail little girl.' It was indeed wonderful how the public had come to know about her. The omnibus conductors used to touch their hats as she drove past, in order to get an answering smile from the pale little face.

I hope my readers will not think that I have said too much about our little girl. There are, thank God, countless other beautiful child characters, and many may justly think that their own children are not less worthy of commemoration. But let what I have written be taken as a reverent tribute to the child nature, which our Saviour loved and bade us imitate. At a time when so much of our literature is strangely blind to the glory and excellence of human nature at its best, I do not think that we can be blamed for making known what we have ourselves seen of the beauty of holiness in a short life, and for showing, as the letters which I have quoted and many other like them have shown, how many sweet natures there are in the world, swift to recognise and love that beauty when they see it in another. Some will, I hope, be reminded of children who, like our little daughter, have been lent them for a time and then taken home into the presence of the Lord of little children. For we ought to remember them, and ' keep our memory green ' for those sad but blessed experiences of our human lot. Some may perhaps have the same feeling that we have, that there may be a wonderful completeness in a life which only lasted a few years. ' She, being made perfect in a short time, fulfilled a long time, for her soul was dear to the Lord.'

39 CHRISTIAN SAINTLINESS—II

It is one of the characteristics of our time, that even those who have no definite Christian faith themselves are able to a large extent to sympathise with and admire the Christian saint. The best life of St. Bernard was written by Cotter Morison, who in the *Service of Man* made a bitter attack upon nearly all that we mean by Christianity. The best life of St. Francis of Assisi is by Sabatier, who if he were in this country would probably be a Unitarian. One of the best lives of St. Teresa is by Mrs. Cunningham Graham, who does not write as a believer. It is something to be thankful for, that the beauty of holiness should be recognised even by those who stand outside the Christian pale, and ungrudgingly admitted.

40   The characteristics of a saint, as we understand them, are purely moral; but the saint differs from the virtuous man in possessing a strain of heroism, of enthusiasm, and of spontaneity, in his moral conduct.

41   I confess that I ardently desire to see a revival of the best Evangelical type of Christian saintliness in our generation. I deplore the decay of the old English Sunday, which may have been an infliction to children, but which was a day of true rest, recollection, and home affection for the busy adult. The modern weekly bank holiday is a very poor substitute. And a touch of austerity for the sake of austerity—a preference for the simple, unwasteful life, is grievously needed. The new Evangelicalism need not be hostile to Art, it need not be prim, morose, or dowdy; but it should be willing to endure hardness, not in order to keep Church rules—'the tradition of the elders'— nor to help the poor, but from a conviction that the simple life is the right life for a Christian, who is a pilgrim and a soldier on active service. The moral

value and dignity of work well done, for its own sake, is another lesson which our generation is forgetting, and of which it should be reminded. Of the value of the life of personal piety and devotion to Jesus Christ, of habitual and unashamed resort to prayer and praise, and childlike trust that all things, great and little, are ordered for the best, there is no need that I should speak to you.

42 It is absolutely essential, if the Church is to take its proper place in the twentieth century, that some of our saints should be thinkers, and some of our thinkers saints. It is for the Liberal Churchman to show in his own life that there is no necessary connection between intellectual candour or courage and religious lukewarmness or want of spirituality. Is it too much to hope that liberal theology may have its own distinctive type of saint, who may discharge in the twentieth century much the same high and noble function that moral philosophy discharged in the later age of antiquity? I picture to myself a highly cultivated man, austerely simple in his manner of life, but no ascetic; a man who, *because* his own citizenship is in heaven, and his deepest life hid with Christ in God, longs with a prophet's yearning to reform human society according to the pattern showed him in the Mount; who believes that the Church of England has no interests except the highest welfare of the people of England; who knows that the river of truth receives affluents from every side, and will therefore learn readily from all who are able to teach him; who

brings out of his treasury things new and old, old things made new, and new things that were true before the world was; the pioneer of that nobler civilisation, that purer Christianity, which we dream of as destined one day to renew the youth of the nations of the West. Our own part in this work will depend on the manner in which we take heed to ourselves and to our teaching, and first and foremost, to *ourselves*.

43   There is after all something in Christian saintliness which eludes analysis. For saintliness is the partial expression, the reflection in the external life of the hidden man of the heart, who is not fully known even by the saint himself; and it is always imperfect, because it is always going on to perfection. I will not have my portrait painted, said a holy man; for which man do you want to paint ? One of them is not worth painting, and the other is not finished yet.

44 PRAYER

The life of prayer is the Christ-life, the life of which Christ is at once the source, the dynamic, and the goal. It is the life which He lived on earth, and which He continues to live in the hearts of Christians. It may be our life if we will. Do not let us be afraid that our practical usefulness will suffer if we think too much of God and too little of our work. The best teacher is he who can say : ' For their sakes I consecrate or sanctify myself.' Religion is caught rather than taught ; it is the religious teacher, not the religious lesson, that helps the pupil to believe. Prayer naturally, spontaneously, issues in action. Action is the normal completion of the act of will which begins as prayer. That action is not always external, but it is always some kind of effective energy. The true Christian will never be tempted to imitate the ' Hermit ' of Parnell's poem, of whom it was said, ' Prayer all his business, all his pleasure praise ' ; for he would soon find that such prayers and praises are a very poor sort of devotion, and that he who so lives is on the way to be a very poor sort of saint. The true scholar who, as has been said, ' goes to his desk as to an altar,' will do his work better, not worse, than he who does not consecrate his daily work by prayer.

45   No spiritual act is complete till it has been first prayed and then done. And after that comes the call to a purer prayer and a nobler act. Such is the spiral stair by which man may ascend to heaven.

46   The suggestion that in prayer we only hear the echo of our own voices is ridiculous to any one who has prayed. The religious experience claims to be a direct experience of ultimate spiritual reality, in exactly the same way in which our eyes tell us that this chapel is enclosed by walls which do not exist only in our imagination. If a man chooses to be a solipsist or a subjective idealist, I do not know that we can dislodge him from his theoretical position. But most of us are content to believe our bodily eyes, and *a fortiori* we

should be content to accept the evidence of the eye of the soul.

Whoso hath felt the vision of the Highest
    Cannot confound nor doubt Him nor deny ;
Yea, with one voice though thou, O world, deniest,
    Stand thou on that side, for on this am I.

Who that one moment has the least descried Him
    Dimly and faintly, hidden and afar,
Doth not despise all excellence beside Him,
    Pleasures and powers that are not and that are,—

Yea, amid all men bear himself thereafter,
    Smit with a solemn and a sweet surprise,
Dumb to their scorn, and turning on their laughter
    Only the dominance of earnest eyes ?

47   Prayer always lifts us above the psychic life, with its self-centredness and distractions. And is it not a matter of experience, that whenever we feel ourselves lifted above this psychic life—whenever we can put aside that psychic classification of experience into ' things which help me ' and ' things which thwart me ' —whenever we are able for a time to view things objectively, impersonally, theocentrically, we feel at once that we are breathing a larger and more wholesome air, and that a glow of health and joy permeates our whole being ?

48 FAITH

Faith is an act of self-consecration, in which the will, the intellect, and the affections all have their place. It is the resolve to live as if certain things were true,

in the confident assurance that they are true, and that
we shall one day find out for ourselves that they are
true. The process of verification begins as soon as we
have honestly set out to climb. We ourselves change,
and the world changes to our sight. The landscape
opens out more and more as we get further up the
hill.

49 Faith is a kind of climbing instinct, which draws us
upward and onward. It is at first quite vague and
undifferentiated, and partly subconscious. Then it
takes shape as a homage to, and craving after, God, who
shines as a triple constellation in the spiritual firmament, as the Source of the Good, the True, and the
Beautiful. The God of Faith is revealed to us under
these three attributes. As parts of God's nature they
are eternal facts. Whatever is real and permanent in
the world that we know, partakes in these qualities.
The triple star shines ever above us, with light blended
yet distinct. It shines above us, and it shines within
us, too. The inner light is the light of Faith, and the
outer light is the light of Grace ; and these two are
only the two sides—the human and the divine aspects
—of the same illumination. It comes from God ; but
it does not come—it could not come—into us from
outside. It is the Spirit of God within us that discerns
and bears witness to the Spirit of God outside us.

50 The normal movement of Faith is double, like the
action of the valves of the heart. Our whole nature
is ennobled and enhanced as we try to follow the gleam,

dimly perceived perhaps, but deeply believed in. And this enrichment takes the double form of expansion and concentration. Let us never forget that one is as necessary as the other. If we read the writings of the mystics, we shall find that nearly all the stress is laid on concentration. We are to draw all things into one, detaching ourselves from whatever we cannot translate into a symbol of the divine. ' Go not forth,' they say to us ; ' return into thyself ; in the inner man is the habitation of truth.' This is indeed a lesson that we have to learn. The inner chamber must be made pure for the divine Guest. We are not to be careful and troubled about many things, when one thing is needful. Prayer and meditation will teach us much that we cannot learn in any other way. If we cannot find God, it is perhaps because He is at home, while we are abroad ; He is ready for us, while we are too busy to attend to Him.

51 Such, then, is Faith is its essence—it is the human aspect of divine Grace. This alone is primary. All else, creeds, dogmas, philosophies, moralities, ritual and cultus, are secondary. It is right and natural that our faith should create these forms ; most of us cannot do without them. But they are all Faith's instruments ; they are not the foundation on which Faith is built.

52 THE CHURCH

The history of a Church ought to be a biography of ideals. The Roman Church is in no danger while the

The Church

Catholic saint continues to be held in honour. And what is true of Romanism must also be true of Anglicanism, if the Church of England is to continue to exist as a great institution. There must be a type of character, a spiritual tradition, which is fostered and sheltered by the institution, and which has a natural affinity to that form of Christianity for which the institution stands. The Church of England is in intention, and during the greater part of its history has been in fact, the Church of the English people. The Reformation was an attempt, and a very successful attempt, to adapt the traditions and practices of mediaeval Catholicism to the spirit of the English race, which in the glorious age of Queen Elizabeth awoke to a consciousness of its gifts, its opportunities, and its destiny. But the English character is a very complex one. It contains, as integral elements of its composition, a sturdy individualism, a strong vein of sentimentality, a high estimation of external morality, and a peculiar blend of idealism and practicality, which foreigners, who do not understand it and only observe its results, are apt to miscall hypocrisy. It rejects, on the whole, alien disciplines—the fanatical racialism of the Jew ; the Roman Catholic type of piety, which is at home only in the Latin nations, coming into sharp conflict with the Northern code of honour and fair play, as well as with the Northern homage to material efficiency and the Northern love of comfort ; and not less, the forms which Protestantism took on the Continent—the logical precision of the Genevan theocracy, and the emotional pietism of the Lutheran

Church. No doubt in a mixed population such as ours, individuals may be found in considerable number who have natural affinities to every one of these types; but on the whole, the Church of England has a character of its own, which fits it to be the Church of the English people.

53   No institution has ever had such a magnificent body of devoted servants as the Roman Catholic Church. It is impossible not to feel what a source of strength it is to be one of an army, obeying the principles of a militant organisation. Catholicism has the advantage of the *esprit de corps*, the unquestioning obedience, the prompt self-surrender, which are demanded in brave soldiers. The testimony of impartial observers to the mission work of the Roman Catholics, whether priests or nuns, is very remarkable. There can be no doubt that that Church is still able to produce devoted servants worthy of its old traditions.

54   Even those who have least sympathy with Catholicism cannot help feeling that it is a religion for a gentleman. Dignity and calmness, security and assurance, the absence of anything petty and provincial impart an air of distinction to Catholic piety, which is too often lacking in the smaller Protestant sects.

55   Organised Christianity is at present under a cloud. The Churches have but little influence, and if they had more they would not know what to do with it   But

the rationalistic assumption that the Christian religion is played out is quite out of date and betrays a complete absence of the historical sense. Religious institutions are by far the toughest and most long-lived of all human associations. Nothing could destroy the Christian Churches except the complete decay and submergence of the white race, a most improbable contingency. Ages of belief and of unbelief follow each other, and perhaps both are wrongly named. And if the Churches seem fairly secure, much more so is the revelation of which they are the guardians. With the added experience of nearly two thousand years, the modern man can repeat the words of St. Paul, that ' other foundation can no man lay save that which is laid,' that is to say, ' Christ the same yesterday, to-day, and for ever.'

56   We must wait in patience for the coming of the wise master-builders who will construct a more truly Catholic Church out of the fragments of the old, with the help of the material now being collected by philosophers, psychologists, historians, and scientists of all creeds and countries. When the time comes for this building to rise, the contributions of the Catholic Modernists will not be described as wood, hay, or stubble. They have done valuable service to Biblical criticism, and in other branches, which will be always recognised. But the building will not (we venture to prophesy) be erected on their plan, nor by their Church. History shows few examples of the rejuvenescence of decayed autocracies. Nor is our generation likely to see much

of the reconstruction. The churches, as institutions, will continue for some time to show apparent weakness; and other moralising and civilising agencies will do much of their work. But, since there never has been a time when the character of Christ and the ethics which he taught have been held in higher honour than the present, there is every reason to believe that the next 'Age of Faith' when it comes, will be of a more genuinely Christian type than the last.

57   Meanwhile, the special work assigned to the Church of England would seem to be the development of a *Johannine* Christianity, which shall be both Catholic and Evangelical without being either Roman or Protestant. It has been abundantly proved that neither Romanism nor Protestantism, regarded as alternatives, possesses enough of the truth to satisfy the religious needs of the present day. But is it not probable that, as the theology of the Fourth Gospel acted as a reconciling principle between the opposing sections in the early Church, so it may be found to contain the teaching which is most needed by both parties in our own communion ? In St. John and St. Paul we find all the principles of a sound and sober Christian Mysticism ; and it is to these 'fresh springs' of the spiritual life that we must turn, if the Church is to renew her youth.

58 REUNION

The time may come—and I hope will come—when

the immense majority of English Christians may be content to worship under the same roof; but assuredly we shall not live to see it, and overtures to the other Protestant bodies seem to me, I regret to say, quite premature.

Reunion then, in the sense of fusion with any other Church or Churches, is not a question of practical politics. But let us remember that all good Christians in England are our brethren and have a claim to individual recognition as good Christians. I entirely agree with the words—I forget who uttered them— that the idea of a common Christianity, behind all denominational loyalties, is one which we should steadily hold before ourselves, and encourage by every means in our power.

Let us further remember, with a view to hastening the happy healing of our unhappy divisions—which we pray and hope for, but shall not live to see—how very partial, how very external, almost superficial, those divisions are. Has the Church of Christ ever been divided in the chambers where men shut their door and pray to their Father who is in secret ? Do we not all pray the same prayers—at least the same prayer of prayers ? Has it ever been divided in the service of praise and thanksgiving ? How many of us know or care which hymns in ' Ancient and Modern ' were written by Roman Catholics, which by Anglicans, and which by Dissenters ? Has it ever been divided in the shelves where we keep our books of devotion ? The ' Imitation of Christ,' Taylor's ' Holy Living and Dying,' ' The Counsels of Father

John Sergieff of Cronstadt,' Penn's 'No Cross no Crown' jostle each other near our bedhead, and do not quarrel. The mystics all tell the same tale. They have climbed the same mountain, and their witness agrees together. All ages, denominations, and languages are blended harmoniously on that Jacob's ladder which scales the heavens in far other fashion than is ever dreamed of by the builders of Babel. Has Christendom ever been divided in the world of letters? Do not Biblical scholars, historians, philosophers forget their denominational differences, and work side by side in the cause of truth? Lastly, are we divided in philanthropy and social service? Do we not unite, naturally and spontaneously, in the warfare against vice, crime, and injustice? These are no slight bonds of union. They embrace by far the greater part of our life as children of God and brethren of each other. Is it not much that we already have in common? Let us not magnify the institutional barriers which part us at public worship, but at no other times. If the Church of the future will, as we hope, be co-extensive with all who love the Lord Jesus Christ in incorruptness; if this is the goal towards which we are moving, however slowly; if this is the idea of the Church which already exists in the mind of God as a fact; let us press forward thither in heart and mind; let us anticipate that which will surely come to pass, and which, when it has come to pass, will make what is now the present appear in quite a new light; let us keep that 'ideal of a Christian Church' ever before us, gazing upon it with that eye of faith which gives substance to things hoped for, and conviction to things not seen.

59 The unity of Christendom which alone we can desire and rationally seek to promote is not the unity of a world-wide centralised government, but unity of spirit based on a common faith and a common desire to see the Kingdom of God, which is ' righteousness and peace and joy in the Holy Ghost,' established on earth. There will be diversities of gifts, but the same Spirit; differences of ecclesiastical organisation, but the same Lord. We must not expect that India, China, and Japan, if they ever adopt Christianity, will be European Christians. They have their ancient traditions, unlike the Graeco-Roman traditions which formed Catholicism; they must build their national churches upon these, in complete independence.

The sole bond of a spiritually united Christendom is the Person and the Gospel of the Divine Founder.

PART II

THE ETERNAL VALUES

60 THE world is a hymn sung by the creative Logos to the glory of God the Father. Its objects, so far as we can discern, are the manifestation of the nature of God under His three attributes of Wisdom, Beauty, and Goodness. We call these three attributes of God the Absolute Values. They are absolute because they exist in their own right and cannot be made means to anything else, not even to each other, and because they are eternal and unchangeable. We call them values because they are the subjects of qualitative judgments; they cannot be measured or given quantitative equivalents. They are, we say, spiritual goods, in which we may participate in proportion to our own spiritual growth. We do not make them; they are above us. It is rather they that make us immortal and blessed if we can lay hold of them and live in them.

61 The eternal Values are not entirely separate from each other; they are a triple star, and we shall be harmoniously developed men in proportion as we can make our own something of what the saint, the scientist, and the artist respectively find in their experience of life.

62   It is plain, therefore, that no critical results can
touch religious values, but only the casket in which
they are enshrined.   Whatever has value in God's
sight is safe for evermore ; and we are safe in so far
as we attach ourselves to what is precious in His eyes.

63   The art of living is not best understood by highly
industrialised communities, where men are too busy
to think, and where the cult of efficiency makes them
reluctant to waste time, as they put it, by considering
whether their standards of value correspond with the
nature of things and with their own best selves.   But
we ought not to evade these questions.   For it is an
unpleasant reflection that the same motives which
make big business hostile to sensual gratifications must
make it antagonistic to all the higher interests of life—
to art, science, philosophy, and religion.   For all these
are in one way like drink—they ' make men desire
fewer things.'   A philosopher was once asked by a
vulgar fellow whether his philosophy had ever brought
him in any money.   The answer, intended to be
intelligible to the questioner, was : ' It has saved me
a great many expenses.'   ' Consumptionism ' plainly
has no use for philosophy !

64   Now these mental and moral possessions are their
own reward.   They cannot, like earthly possessions,
be taken away from us.   For those who know what
they are worth, the world is a much brighter place than
for those who think that a man's life consisteth in the
abundance of the things which he possesseth.   The

man whose 'mind to him a kingdom is' does not complain much of the injustices of life. Still less does the true Christian complain. He has found the joy that no man taketh from him. This world is not a bad place in his eyes, because he finds it full of love and beauty and wisdom. He knows that it is God's world, even though, in sad times like this, it seems to be 'full of darkness and cruel habitations.' Amid all the horrors of war and strife he sees the pure gold of love and heroism and devotion shining brightly.

65   The right to speak about the eternal values—the right even to believe in them—must be earned by strict self-discipline. 'If anyone is willing to do His will, he shall know of the doctrine.' 'Blessed are the pure in heart, for they shall see God.' In proportion as we acclimatise ourselves to the pure and fine air of the spiritual world, the difficulties and puzzles of popular eschatology fade away into comparative insignificance.

66 LOVE

All human love is a holy thing, the holiest thing in our experience. It is the chief mode of initiation into the mysteries of the divine life, the most direct point of contact with the nature of our Creator. 'He prayeth best who loveth best.' Pure affection 'abides' in a sense in which nothing else abides. It is rooted in the eternal, and cannot be destroyed by any of the changes and chances of mortal life. It is a relation between immortal spirits, which in the eternal world are united together solely by likeness of nature ; so that death not only makes no break in the ties of pure affection, but liberates it from adventitious obstacles which at present only impede its free action and dull its radiance. When we know even as we are known, we shall know our friends and be known by them, to a degree which we cannot even imagine now.

67 Love, whether in its most exalted form as the love between husband and wife, or in the less ardent experience of affection and sympathy, unlocks the doors of our prison-house and reveals to us something of the breadth and length and depth and height of the spiritual world which surrounds us. In various degrees, all cordial human intercourse is a liberation and an enhancement of our personality ; it is a channel of revelation.

68 The spiritualising power of human love is the redeeming principle in many sordid lives. Teutonic civilisation, which derives half of its restless energy from ideals which are essentially anti-Christian, and tastes which are radically barbarous, is prevented from sinking into moral materialism by its high standard of domestic life. The sweet influences of the home deprive even mammon-worship of half its grossness and of some fraction of its evil. As a school-master to bring men and women to Christ, natural affection is without a rival. It is in the truest sense a symbol of our union with Him from whom every family in heaven and earth is named.

69 Hatred towards any human being cannot exist in the same heart as love to God.

70 The fact that human love or sympathy is the guide who conducts us to the heart of life, revealing to us God and Nature and ourselves, is proof that part of our life is bound up with the life of the world, and that if we live in these our true relations we shall not entirely die so long as human beings remain alive upon this earth. The progress of the race, the diminution of sin and misery, the advancing Kingdom of Christ on earth,—these are matters in which we have a *personal* interest. The strong desire that we feel— and the best of us feel it most strongly—that the human race may be better, wiser, and happier in the future than they are now or have been in the past, is neither due to a false association of ideas nor to pure unselfishness. There is a sense in which death would not be the end of everything for us, even though in this life only we had hope in Christ.

71 BEAUTY

The Beauty of the world, as many have felt, is the strongest evidence we have of the goodness and benevolence of the Creator. Not, of course, that the world was made beautiful for our sakes. It is beautiful because its Author is beautiful; and we should remember that when the old writers spoke of God as the Author of nature, they used the word in much the same sense as if we said that a man was the author of his own photograph. But we are allowed to see and enjoy beauty, although the gift cannot be proved to promote our own survival. It looks like a free gift of God. Beauty is a general quality of nature, and not only of organic nature; crystals are very beautiful. As in the case of the other ultimate values, the emotion of beauty is aroused by the meeting of mind and its object; and not only must the object be beautiful; the perceiving mind must also be beautiful and healthy. The vile or vulgar mind not only cannot discern beauty; it is a great destroyer of beauty everywhere.

The love of beauty is super-personal and disinterested, like all the spiritual values; it promotes common enjoyment and social sympathy. Unquestionably it is one of the three ultimate values, ranking with Goodness and Truth.

72 According to Plotinus, when we pass from visible and audible beauty to the beauty which the Soul perceives without the help of the senses, we must remember that we can only perceive what is akin to ourselves—there is such a thing as soul-blindness. Incorporeal things are beautiful when they make us love them. But what constitutes their beauty? Negatively, it is the absence of impure admixture. An ugly character is soiled by base passions; it is like a body caked with mud; in order to restore its natural grace it must be scraped and cleansed. This is why it has been said that all the virtues are a purification. The purified soul becomes a form, a meaning, wholly spiritual and incorporeal. The true beauty of the Soul is to be

made like to God. The good and the beautiful are the same, and the ugly and the bad are the same. The Soul becomes beautiful through Spirit; other things, such as actions and studies, are beautiful through Soul which gives them form. The Soul too gives to bodies all the beauty which they are able to receive.

73 JOY

Joy is the emotional experience which our kind Father in heaven has attached to the discharge of the most fundamental of all the higher activities—namely, those of inner growth and outer creativeness. Joy is the triumph of *life*; it is the sign that we are living our true life as spiritual beings. We are sent into the world to become something and to make something. The two are in practice so closely connected as to be almost inseparable. Our personality expands by creativeness, and creates spontaneously as it expands. Joy is the signal that we are spiritually alive and active. Wherever joy is, creation has been; and the richer the creation, the deeper the joy.

74   There are few purer sources of happiness than the consciousness of having actually made or produced something good of its kind. Whether the product be useful, or beautiful, it is the same. If it was worth doing, and if we have done it, or rather, are doing it, joy results. But the joy is greater in proportion to the spiritual value of the thing produced. A great

work of art, or a great scientific discovery, gives greater joy to its maker than a work of merely technical or mechanical skill. And the fulfilment of the prophetic and priestly function of bringing a human soul to the knowledge of God and the service of man gives perhaps the deepest joy of all.

75   Christian joy is a happiness which has passed through and overcome suffering, and has attained to life through the gate of death.

76 BOREDOM

I want you to think earnestly of the witness which Joy on the one hand, and its antithesis, Boredom, on the other, bear to the duty and happiness of creative work, that is to say, real work, on however small a scale. The happy people are those who are producing something; the bored people are those who are consuming much and producing nothing. If you want to see examples of the latter class, look in at the bow-window of a London Club in the morning, or at the carriages in Hyde Park towards the end of the season. While we are still on our probation, God punishes the useless by giving them pleasure without joy; and very wearisome they find it. We are all given the choice whether we will crawl or climb. Parasitism is open to us, if we like. Choose it, and pleasure, that apple of Sodom—may be yours; but you will wholly forfeit joy.

77   Boredom, then, is a certain sign that we are allowing our best faculties to rust in idleness. When people

are bored, they generally look about for a new pleasure, or take a holiday. There is no greater mistake : what they want is some hard piece of work—some productive drudgery. Doctors are fond of sending their fashionable patients to take a rest-cure. In nine cases out of ten, a work-cure would do them far more good.

78 SELF-CONSECRATION

Self-consecration is the most effectual way by which we can serve God in our generation. This is the way in which the torch has been handed on by the long succession of runners since the Gospel of Christ came into the world.

79 The indwelling Spirit of Christ radiates its benign influence as Life, as Light, and as Love. Christ is the eternal principle of life in all that lives. ' That which came into being, in Him was Life, and the Life was the Light of men.' He came ' that we might have Life, and have it more abundantly.' The call of Christ is the call to a more vivid, earnest, strenuous life. It has been said of a great man that he passed through the dream of life as one awake ; and that is what all Christians ought to do. ' Now it is high time to awake out of sleep.' Spiritual wakefulness means concentration of purpose. The world may be divided into those who have a purpose in life, and those who have none, or who fluctuate between several. Few things are more striking than the change which comes over even the outward appearance of a man or woman between youth and old age, according to

whether he or she has or has not a fixed purpose which is being carried out day by day. The face of the man who has found his work shows, in each decade of his life until the failure of his powers, increasing strength and dignity, and even beauty; while the man who lets himself drift shows in every line of his face that his will has been overpowered by disorderly impulses, or has simply abdicated. The portraits of good and great men at various ages, and the faces of those who are neither good nor great, are instructive in this way.

80   What is called 'a narrow sphere' does not matter much. A broad mind is not much cramped by a narrow sphere. Some of the noblest and loftiest lives have been led under the most meagre and depressing conditions. No; it is our personal defects that hamper us; our mental sluggishness and our want of sympathy; yes, and the heavy burdens which we have to carry, in the sins which do most easily beset us. These are the chains with which we are tied and bound. But I think we are as much inclined to underrate our possibilities as to overrate our achievements.

81   There is no self-expenditure without self-enrichment, no self-enrichment without self-expenditure.

PART III

SOCIOLOGY

82 CIVILISATION

IF I were asked to state in one word the cause of the failure of our civilisation, I should answer ' Secularism.' There must surely be some very deep ground for the universal discontent and *malaise* which have overtaken Western civilisation. There is but little happiness and content anywhere, and the reason is that we have lost faith in the values which should be the motive force of social life. Capitalism is in danger, not so much from the envious attacks of the unpropertied, as from the decay of that Puritan asceticism which was its creator. The glory of subduing the earth and producing something—no matter what—on a large scale ; the accumulation of wealth, not for enjoyment, but as the means of increased power and the instrument of new enterprise—this conception of a worthy and God-fearing life no longer appeals to men as it did. The capitalist now is too often an idler or a gambler, and as such he can justify his existence neither to himself nor to others. The working-man also has too often no pride and no conscience in his work. He works in the spirit of a slave, grudgingly and bitterly, and then ascribes his unhappiness to the conditions of his employment. He is becoming well educated ; but he twists everything round, even religion, to his alleged economic griev- ances, and loses sight of higher interests. Industrialism drags on, because the alternative is starvation ; but the life and joy have gone out of it, and it seems likely to pass into a state of gradual decay. Civilisation presents the spectacle of a mighty tree which is dying at the roots. When masses of men begin to ask simultaneously ' Is it all worth while ? What is the use of this great Babylon that we have builded ? ' we are reminded that the mediaeval casuists classified *acedia*, which is just this temper, among the seven deadly sins. We had almost forgotten *acedia*, and few know the meaning of the word ; but it is at the bottom of the diseases from which we are suffering— the frivolous and joyless emptiness of life among the rich, and the bitter discontent of the hand-workers.

83   I believe that the dissatisfaction with things as they are is caused not only by the failure of nineteenth-century civilisation, but partly also by its success. We no longer wish to progress on those lines if we could. Our apocalyptic dream is vanishing into thin air. It may be that the industrial revolution which began in the reign of George III has produced most of its fruits, and has had its day. We may have to look forward to such a change as is imagined by Anatole France at the end of his ' Isle of the Penguins,' when, after an orgy of revolution and destruction, we shall slide back into the quiet rural life of the early modern period. If so, the authors of the revolution will have

cut their own throats, for there can be no great manu-
facturing towns in such a society. The race will have
tried a great experiment, and will have rejected it
as unsatisfying. We shall have added something to
our experience. Fontenelle exclaimed, ' How many
foolish things we should say now, if the ancients had
not said them all before us ! ' Fools are not so much
afraid of plagiarism as this Frenchman supposed ;
but it is true that ' Eventu rerum stolidi didicere
magistro.'

84   The chief danger to the white man arises from his
arrogant contempt for other races, a contempt which
in some lands is mixed with fear and hatred, and which
has provoked fear and hatred in return. Europeans
have recently enjoyed an unfair advantage over their
rivals, which they have abused without the slightest
regard for justice and fair play. This advantage will
not be theirs in the future ; they will have to compete
on equal terms with nations schooled by adversity and
winnowed by the hard struggle for existence. Victory
will go to the races which are best equipped for that
kind of competition ; and it may well be that a
modified caste system, not rigid, as in India, but such
as prevailed till lately in Europe, may prove to have a
greater survival value than either democracy or social-
ism, which in its present form desires to keep the whole
population as nearly as possible on the same level.
An English poet has given his opinion that fifty years
of Europe are better than a cycle of Cathay. But the
future may show that the European is a good sprinter

and a bad stayer. It is better to be a hare than a tortoise; but it is better to be a live tortoise than a dead hare.

85   Behind the problem of our own future rises the great question whether any nation which aims at being a working-man's paradise can long flourish. Civilisation hitherto has always been based on great inequality. It has been the culture of a limited class, which has given its character to the national life, but has not attempted to raise the whole people to the same level. Some civilisations have decayed because the privileged class, obeying a law which seems to be almost invariable, have died out, and the masses have been unable to perpetuate a culture which they never shared.

86 PROGRESS

Our optimists have not made it clear to themselves or others what they mean by progress, and we may suspect that the vagueness of the idea is one of its attractions. There has been no physical progress in our species for many thousands of years. The Cro-Magnon race, which lived perhaps twenty thousand years ago, was at least equal to any modern people in size and strength; the ancient Greeks were, I suppose, handsomer and better formed than we are; and some unprogressive races, such as the Zulus, Samoans, and Tahitians, are envied by Europeans for either strength or beauty. Although it seems not to be true that the sight and hearing of civilised peoples are inferior to those of savages, we have certainly lost our natural weapons, which from one point of view is a mark of degeneracy. Mentally, we are now told that the men of the Old Stone Age, ugly as most of them must have been, had as large brains as ours ; and he would be a bold man who should claim that we are intellectually equal to the Athenians or superior to the Romans. The question of moral improvement is much more difficult. Until the Great War few would have disputed that civilised man had become much more humane, much more sensitive to the sufferings of others, and so more just, more self-controlled, and less brutal in his pleasures and in his resentments. The habitual honesty of the Western European might also have been contrasted with the rascality of inferior races in the past and present. It was often forgotten that, if progress means the improvement of human nature itself, the question to be asked is whether the modern civilised man behaves better in the same circumstances than his ancestor would have done. Absence of temptation may produce an appearance of improvement ; but this is hardly what we mean by progress, and there is an old saying that the Devil has a clever trick of pretending to be dead. It seems to me very doubtful whether, when we are exposed to the same temptations, we are more humane or more sympathetic or juster or less brutal than the ancients.

87   I do not wish to be misunderstood as denying the possibility of temporal progress. There will undoubtedly be pleasanter times to live in than the twentieth century. Civilisation is at present in very

rough water ; after a time it will probably enter a calm channel, when most people will, for a time, be more or less contented. Accumulated experience may enable mankind to avoid some dangers and some mistakes. Science will put into the hands of our grandchildren the means to diminish the amount of irksome toil, though it will also provide the means of mutual extermination on a hitherto unexampled scale. It is just possible that our successors may care enough for posterity to bring about, by selective breeding, a real improvement in the human stock. These reflections give us a ground for reasonable, if chastened, hopefulness. But they have little or nothing to do with the Christian faith, which makes no temporal promises.

88   Nor is it quite correct to deny all progress within the historical period. There are, after all, horrors described in the Old Testament, in Greek history, in Roman history, in mediaeval history, which only the Bolsheviks have rivalled, and which indicate a degree of depravity which we may perhaps hope that civilised humanity has outgrown. And if there has been perceptible progress in the last two thousand years, the improvement may be considerable in the next ten thousand, a small fraction, probably, of the whole life of the species. The Soul of the race is no demon, but a child with great possibilities. It is capable of what it has already achieved in the noblest human lives, and the character which it has accepted as the perfect realisation of the human ideal is the character of Christ.

89   The votaries of progress mistake the flowing tide
for the river of eternity, and when the tide turns they
are likely to be left stranded like the corks and scraps
of seaweed which mark the high-water line. This
has already happened, though few realise it.

90   For individuals the path of progress is always open;
but, as Hesiod told us long before the Sermon on the
Mount, it is a narrow path, steep and difficult,
especially at first. There will never be a crowd
gathered round this gate; ' few there be that find it.'
For this reason, we must cut down our hopes for our
nation, for Europe, and for humanity at large, to
a very modest and humble aspiration. We have no
millennium to look forward to; but neither need
we fear any protracted or widespread retrogression.
There will be new types of achievement which will
enrich the experience of the race; and from time to
time, in the long vista which science seems to promise
us, there will be new flowering-times of genius and
virtue, not less glorious than the age of Sophocles or
the age of Shakespeare. They will not merely repeat
the triumphs of the past, but will add new varieties
to the achievements of the human mind.

91   The strange notion is widely held that this doctrine
of temporal progress is part of the Christian religion.
But I cannot find a trace of it in the Gospels. The
idea of a long vista of future history, whether marked
by advance or decline, is wholly foreign to the purview
of Christ and His Apostles. Whatever Christ Himself

believed and taught about the Kingdom of God, He allowed His disciples to believe that it was to be brought in, within a few years, by supernatural agency. If He had ever spoken about the upward progress of the human race, they could not have retained their patriotic dreams of a national restoration within their own lifetime, by a miracle which was to bring the present world-order to an end.

Even more decisive is the uniform tenor of His language about what His disciples have to expect in this world. They and their message were to be rejected as their Master and His message were rejected. ' If they have called the Master of the house Beelzebub, how much more them of his household ? ' There are many sayings of this kind, and none which contradict them. As if to cut off all dreams of a final victory for the Church, He says ' When the Son of Man cometh, shall he find faith on the earth ? ' No other leader was ever half so candid as this. He promises nothing in this life, except the privilege of bearing the cross after Him.

This, which, whether we like it or no, is the real teaching of the Gospels, casts a deadly chill on what passes for Christianity among the majority. We do not like to hear that ' the world passeth away and the lust thereof.' Science, of course, tells us the same, but we shut our ears to Christ and to our astronomers impartially. And yet I think this secularist dogma is dying, as I should be glad to think that all the rest of the poisonous legacy of Rousseau was dying. It must be plain to every thinking man that there is no natural tendency such as this belief postulates, and that earthly life, whether for the race or the individual, is given ' to none in perpetuity, to all in usufruct.'

92 SOCIAL UNREST

Social unrest is a disease of town-life. Wherever the conditions which create the great modern city exist, we find revolutionary agitation. It has spread to Barcelona, to Buenos Ayres, and to Osaka, in the wake of the factory. The inhabitants of the large town do not envy the countryman and would not change with him. But, unknown to themselves, they are leading an unnatural life, cut off from the kindly and wholesome influences of nature, surrounded by vulgarity and ugliness, with no traditions, no loyalties, no culture, and no religion. We seldom reflect on the strangeness of the fact that the modern working-man has few or no superstitions. At other times the masses have evolved for themselves some picturesque nature-religion, some pious ancestor-worship, some cult of saints or heroes, some stories of fairies, ghosts, or demons, and a mass of quaint superstitions, genial or frightening. The modern town-dweller has no God and no Devil; he lives without awe, without admiration, without fear. Whatever we may think about these beliefs, it is not natural for men and women to be without them. The life of the town artisan who works in a factory is a life to which the human organism has not adapted itself; it is an unwholesome and unnatural condition. Hence, probably, comes

66

the *malaise* which makes him think that any radical change must be for the better.

Whatever the cause of the disease may be (and I do not pretend that the conditions of urban life are an adequate explanation) the malady is there, and will probably prove fatal to our civilisation.

93   The community at large must realise that there are many non-economic causes of discontent and rebellion, and that these are easier to remedy than the economic difficulties. Whatever remains from the habits of past generations of arrogance and exclusiveness in social intercourse should be done away with. The notion that one calling is intrinsically more honourable than another (except as involving a higher degree of unremunerated service) should be repudiated. Something should be done to diminish the local isolation in which the upper, middle, and lower classes live, each in its own quarter of the town. Above all, perhaps, no investigation can be too thorough into the reasons which make even a moderate day's work, under modern conditions, disagreeable to the worker.

94   I want to remind you and myself, that whatever may be the issue of all the manifold critical, historical, ecclesiastical, political, economic problems that clamour for solution and make our life so unrestful, the foundation of God standeth sure; the things that cannot be shaken remain. As soon as we forget this, as we do forget it too often, the outlook becomes so disquieting that it is hard to keep our courage up.

For it so happens that just at a time when everything shakeable is being shaken, when all authorities and all traditions are being thrown into the melting-pot, just when more than at other times we crave for some wise and strong leadership, we are suffering from one of those mysterious eclipses of genius which often follow periods of great energy and activity.

95 MIDDLE CLASSES

In England we can only say that the golden age of the upper middle class, who in the nineteenth century enjoyed great good fortune, has now come to an end.

96 The destruction of the upper and professional classes by taxation directed expressly against them has already begun, and this victimisation is certain to become more and more acute, till these classes are practically extinguished. The old aristocracy showed a tendency to decay even when they were unduly favoured by legislation, and a little more pressure will drive them to voluntary sterility and extermination. Even more to be regretted is the doom of the professional aristocracy, a caste almost peculiar to our country. These families can often show longer, and usually much better pedigrees than the peerage ; the persistence of marked ability in many of them, for several generations, is the delight of the eugenist. They are perhaps the best specimens of humanity to be found in any country of the world. Yet they have no prospects except to be gradually harassed out of existence, like the *curiales* of the later Roman Empire.

97   There is not really the slightest doubt that whatever tests of physical and mental proficiency are chosen,
the children of the upper and middle classes are
intrinsically far better endowed than the children of
unskilled labourers. And it is probable that the
eugenist would place at the top of his list just those
three professions in which the birth-rate is lowest—
the doctors, the ministers of religion, and the teachers.

No doubt there is something to be said on the other
side. Fecundity seems to be connected with poverty,
not with intellectual inferiority. If, therefore, political
changes depress the most gifted stocks into extreme
poverty, and heap wealth on trade union officials and
political agitators who are usually very undesirable
citizens, the former class may be induced to increase,
the latter to die out. Again, social position once
gained has been so stable in England that even if the
founder of a family was an able man, his descendants
may be below the average. Thirdly, it may be
disputed whether the qualities which lead to the
acquisition of wealth are very desirable in a State
which wishes to cultivate mutual helpfulness and
unselfishness. But when all has been said, the
dysgenic tendency of modern civilisation is an undeni-
able and an exceedingly serious fact. The burdens
of civilised life grow heavier in each generation, and
the backs that are to bear them are likely to grow
steadily weaker. Applied eugenics might remedy the
evil, when more is known about the laws of heredity
than has yet been established with any certainty;
but a race that is deteriorating biologically is most

unlikely to take far-sighted views about its own future. The Greeks in the age of Plato and Aristotle could do so; but intellectually we are far behind the Athenians of the fourth and fifth centuries before Christ.

98   The maxim, 'Play the game,' may seem to the German childish, to the Frenchman foolishness; but, rightly applied, it is the foundation of all that is best in the English character, and it is the real reason why we have been successful in foreign politics and in governing backward races. Power has now passed to a class which has not been trained in these ideas; and if our administrative posts cease to be staffed by public school men, who instinctively 'play the game,' or by those who have learned their traditions, I believe that the end of our national greatness will not be far off. For this reason I earnestly hope that the conservatism which is ingrained in our national character will be able to save our great schools.

99 DEMOCRACY

   Whatever may be truly said about the good sense of a democracy during a great crisis, at ordinary times it does not bring the best men to the top.

100   The democracy is a ready victim to shibboleths and catchwords, as all demagogues know too well. The politician has only to find a fascinating formula; facts and arguments are powerless against it. The art of the demagogue is the art of the parrot; he must utter some senseless catchword again and again, working on the suggestibility of the crowd.

101 A more serious danger is that of vexatious and
inquisitive tyranny. This is exercised partly through
public opinion, a vulgar, impertinent, anonymous
tyrant who deliberately makes life unpleasant for anyone who is not content to be the average man. But
partly it is seen in constant interference with the
legislature and the executive. No one can govern
who cannot afford to be unpopular, and no democratic
official can afford to be unpopular. Sometimes he
has to wink at flagrant injustice and oppression ; at
other times a fanatical agitation compels him to pass
laws which forbid the citizen to indulge perfectly
harmless tastes, or tax him to contribute to the pleasures
of the majority. In many ways a Russian under the
Tsars was far less interfered with than an Englishman
or American or Australian.

The two diseases which are likely to be fatal to
democracy are anarchy and corruption. A democratic
government is almost necessarily weak and timid. A
democracy cannot tolerate a strong executive for fear
of seeing the control pass out of the hands of the mob.
The executive must be unarmed and defenceless.
The result is that it is at the mercy of any violent and
anti-social faction.

102 Democracy is, in fact, a disintegrating force. It is
strong in destruction, and tends to fall to pieces when
the work of demolition (which may of course be a
necessary task) is over. Democracy dissolves communities into individuals and collects them again into
mobs. It pulls up by the roots the social order which

71

civilisation has gradually evolved, and leaves men *déracinés*, as Barrès says in one of his best novels, homeless and friendless, with no place ready for them to fill. It is the opposite extreme to the caste system of India, which, with all its faults, does not seem to breed the European type of *enragé*, the enemy of society as such.

103   But whether we think that the bad in democracy predominates over the good, or the good over the bad, a question which I shall not attempt to decide, the popular balderdash about it corresponds to no real conviction. The upper class has never believed in it ; the middle class has the strongest reasons to hate and fear it. But how about the lower class, in whose interests the whole machine is supposed to have been set going ? The working man has no respect for either democracy or liberty. His whole interest is in transferring the wealth of the minority to his own pocket. There was a time when he thought that universal suffrage would get for him what he desires ; but he has lost all faith in constitutional methods. To levy blackmail on the community, under threats of civil war, seems to him a more expeditious way of gaining his object.

104   The truth is that, at least in this country, the extension of the suffrage was granted before the masses were ready for it ; it was given in the course of the frantic struggle for power between two political factions, neither of which, in the excitement of the party game, cared to look far ahead. Disraeli hoped

to dish the Whigs; the head of his own party soon adorned the same charger. No impartial observer can any longer doubt that Plato's opinion as to the danger of giving the power of the purse to the democracy was quite correct. For two generations or so the political inexperience of the populace was so great that it allowed itself to be dragged into such purely middle-class causes as the campaign against the Church and the House of Lords. But now that it has had time to realise its power and formulate its own demands, the middle-class programme has been dropped, and one thing alone excites enthusiasm, the pillage of the minority, exactly as Plato told us. So entirely does this object dominate all other considerations, that it unites in one predatory horde parties whose political philosophy (if we may dignify it by such a name) ought to place them in diametrically opposite camps. No two types of political thought are more radically opposed to each other than that of the Socialist, for whom the State is everything, and that of the Syndicalist, for whom the State is nothing. But as long as the loot lasts, they are willing to work together. The consequences to the nation may be even more ruinous than could result from absolute monarchy or oligarchy; and, if so, Plato's political insight will once more be justified by the course of history.

105 LEAGUE FOR MUTUAL PROTECTION

The time may come when the educated classes, and those who desire freedom to live as they think right, will find themselves oppressed, not only in their home-life by the tyranny of the trade-unions, but in their souls by the pulpy and mawkish emotionalism of herd-morality. Then a league for mutual protection may be formed. If such a society ever comes into being, the following principles are, I think, necessary for its success. First, it must be on a religious basis, since religion has a cohesive force greater than any other bond. The religious basis will be a blend of Christian Platonism and Christian Stoicism, since it must be founded on that faith in absolute spiritual values which is common to Christianity and Platonism, with that sturdy defiance of tyranny and popular folly which was the strength of Stoicism. Next, it must not be affiliated to any religious organisation; otherwise it will certainly be exploited in denominational interests. Thirdly, it must include some purely disciplinary asceticism, such as abstinence from alcohol and tobacco for men, and from costly dresses and jewellery for women. This is necessary, because it is more important to keep out the half-hearted than to increase the number of members. Fourthly, it must prescribe a simple life of duty and discipline, since frugality will be a condition of enjoying self-respect and freedom. Fifthly, it will enjoin the choice of an open-air life in the country, where possible. A whole group of French writers, such as Proudhon, Delacroix, Leconte de Lisle, Flaubert, Leblond, and Faguet agree in attributing our social *malaise* to life in great towns. The lower death-rates of country districts are a hint from nature that they are right. Sixthly, every member must pledge himself to give his best work. Seventhly, there must be provision for community-life, like that of the old monasteries, for both sexes. The members of the society should be encouraged to spend some part of their lives in these institutions, without retiring from the world altogether. Temporary ' retreats ' might be of great value. Intellectual work, including scientific research, could be carried on under very favourable conditions in these lay monasteries and convents, which should contain good libraries and laboratories. Lastly, a distinctive dress, not merely a badge, would probably be essential for members of both sexes.

106 WAR

The notion that frequent war is a healthy tonic for a nation is scarcely tenable. Its dysgenic effect, by eliminating the strongest and healthiest of the population, while leaving the weaklings at home to be the fathers of the next generation, is no new discovery. It has been supported by a succession of men, such as Tenon, Dufau, Foissac, de Lapouge, and Richet in France; Tiedemann and Seeck in Germany; Guerrini in Italy; Kellogg and Starr Jordan in America. The case is indeed overwhelming. The lives destroyed in war are nearly all males, thus disturbing the sex equilibrium of the population; they are in the prime of life, at the age of greatest fecundity; and they are picked from a list out of which from 20 to 30 per cent. have been rejected for physical unfitness. It seems to be proved that the children born in France during the Napoleonic wars were poor and undersized—30 millimetres below the normal height. War combined with religious celibacy to ruin Spain. ' Castile makes men and wastes them,' said a Spanish writer. This sublime and terrible phrase sums up the whole of Spanish history. Schiller was right : ' Immer der Krieg verschlingt die besten.' We in England have suffered from this drain in the past ; we shall suffer much more in the next generation.

> We have fed our sea for a thousand years,
>   And she calls us, still unfed,
> Though there's never a wave of all her waves
>   But marks our English dead.
>
> We have strawed our best to the weed's unrest,
>   To the shark and the sheering gull,
> If blood be the price of admiralty,
>   Lord God, we ha' paid in full.

107   Another cause which may give patriots leisure to turn their thoughts away from war's alarms is that the ' swarming ' period of the European races is coming to an end. The unparalleled increase of population in the first three-quarters of the nineteenth century has been followed by a progressive decrease in the birth-rate, which will begin to tell upon social conditions when the reduction in the death-rate, which has hitherto kept pace with it, shall have reached its natural limit. Europe with a stationary population will be in a much happier condition ; and problems of social reform can then be tackled with some hope of success. Honourable emulation in the arts of life may then take the place of desperate compe-

tition and antagonism. Human lives will begin to have a positive value, and we may even think it fair to honour our saviours more than our destroyers. The effects of past follies will then soon be effaced ; for nations recover much more quickly from wars than from internal disorders. External injuries are rapidly cured ; but ' those wounds heal ill that men do give themselves.' The greatest obstacle to progress is not man's inherited pugnacity, but his incorrigible tendency to parasitism. The true patriot will keep his eye fixed on this, and will dread as the State's worst enemies those citizens who at the top and bottom of the social scale have no other ambition than to hang on and suck the life-blood of the nation.

108   A man may build himself a throne of bayonets, but he cannot sit on it.

109 RECREATION

Everywhere we find the same demand to make life easy, safe, and fool-proof. The fine trees in our public parks are periodically mangled and reduced to the condition of clothes-props by our urban and county councils, because boughs have been known to be blown down in a high wind, or even, in the case of elm-trees, to fall suddenly, and once in two hundred years some fool might be standing under the tree at the moment. Every workman must be insured against every variety of accident, even when it is caused by his own negligence. If a traveller slips on a piece of orange-peel, which he ought to have seen,

in a railway station, or allows his coat to be stolen
under his eyes in a carriage, he brings an action against
the railway company, and wins it. We now demand
to be personally conducted through life, all risks to
be taken by someone else. After a century or two of
this regime we shall all be as helpless as Lord Avebury's
ants, who starved almost to death in sight of food
because they were used to having it put into their
mouths by their slaves.

110   All this may be right, or it may only be inevitable.
But do not let us deceive ourselves. Nature will make
us pay for it. Nature takes away any faculty that is
not used. She is taking away our natural defences,
and has probably added nothing since the beginning
of the historical period to our mental powers. The
powers of grappling with difficulties, and finding our
way out of labyrinths, will soon be lost if we no longer
need it. And after any derangement of our social
order we might come to need it very badly. Besides,
can we look with satisfaction at the completed product
of civilisation, a creature unable to masticate, to write,
or to walk, a mere parasite on the machines that enable him to live? Many would prefer to be savages
if they could have the magnificent physique of the
Zulus or some South Sea Islanders.

111   Walking and riding, two delightful and health-
giving exercises, are becoming extinct. Two hundred
years ago the roads were full of riders, and of pedestrians
who thought nothing of thirty miles a day. The joys

of a long country walk, either solitary or with a friend, are unknown to the younger generation, although there is no more delightful way of spending a spring or summer day.

112   Cricket has had a much longer popularity than football, and it would not be easy to exaggerate the beneficial effect which this noble game has had upon the national character. 'To play cricket' has become a synonym for honourable and straightforward team-play in any relation of life. Unlike football and racing, it has been hardly at all corrupted by betting. It was therefore with great regret that I heard from the captain of a first-class county eleven that the home side has now to be carefully watched, to see that they do not roll the ground in such a manner as to help their own team. But unfairness in these contests is not common. We may still congratulate ourselves that the words of an American Rhodes Scholar are true. Being asked, after a year's residence at Oxford, what struck him most in English university life, he replied : 'What strikes me most is that here are three thousand young men, every one of whom would rather lose a game than play it unfairly.' This spirit of fair play, which in the public schools, at any rate, is absorbed as the most inviolable of traditions, has stood our race in good stead in the professions, and especially in the administration of dependencies, where the obvious desire of the officials to deal justly and see fair play in disputes between natives and Europeans has partly compensated for a want of sympathetic

understanding, which has kept the English strangers in lands of alien culture.

113   It is no accident that the Englishman expresses his deepest moral convictions in the terms of a game. One of our chief contributions to the pleasures of the world is that we have invented most of the good games. The love of play is a very old English characteristic.

114 BETTING AND GAMBLING

The tree is known by its fruits, and the fruits of betting and gambling are wholly bad. The gambler frequently defrauds his creditors, leaves his family ruined, and tries to repair by fraud what he has lost by chance. There are habitual gamblers who are as much slaves to their besetting sin as any opium-eater.

115   The real seriousness of betting and gambling is realised only when we consider of what mental condition they are symptomatic. An utter lack of intelligent interests, a dreary boredom and discontent, an entire want of conscience about the getting and spending of money—these are the only states of mind that could drive anyone to the gambling table or the sporting columns of the newspapers. To the man who has found his vocation this gadfly of boredom and monotony is unknown. When the educated man wants to unstring his bow, there are a dozen more interesting employments of his leisure hours waiting for him.

116   Gambling is a disease of barbarians superficially civilised.

117 RIGHTS OF ANIMALS

The last century produced a discovery nearly as important for ethics as that of the unity of mankind. Darwin and his fellow-workers proved that all life in the world springs from one root, and that the lower animals are literally our distant cousins. There is nothing to be ashamed of in the relationship. But we can hardly suppose that the other animals, if they are able to think, admit our superiority. For we have always treated our poor relations in fur and feathers as if they had no rights at all. We have not only enslaved them, and killed and eaten them, but we have made it one of our chief pleasures to take away their lives, and not infrequently to have tortured them.

118   Our ancestors sinned in ignorance; they were taught (as I deeply regret to say one great Christian Church still teaches) that the world, with all that it contains, was made for man, and that the lower orders of creation have no claims whatever upon us. But we have no longer the excuse of saying that we do not know; we do know that organic life on this planet is all woven of one stuff, and that if we are children of our Heavenly Father, it must be true, as Christ told us, that no sparrow falls to the ground without His care. The new knowledge has revolutionised our ideas of our relations to the other living creatures who share the world with us, and it is our duty to consider

seriously what this knowledge should mean for us in matters of conduct.

119   I believe that the time will come when the sportsman, instead of swaggering about railway-stations as he does now, will be fain to hide his tools, as the golfer who should have been at the front tried to smuggle away his clubs during the war.

120   Deliberate cruelty to our defenceless and beautiful little cousins is surely one of the meanest and most detestable vices of which a human being can be guilty.   In this country direct cruelty to animals is severely punished ; but what is the difference between tearing off a bird's wing yourself, and paying someone else to do it for you ?   Women have no excuse for not knowing how their egret plumes are procured. The hideous story is matter of common knowledge. It is a disgrace to the country of Charles Darwin that such trophies should be exhibited and admired.   The wearers should be made to feel that they are repulsive objects, and not beautiful, as they suppose ; and no time should be lost in making the trade illegal.

121   It is reasonable to infer that God made the world beautiful because beauty is one of His own attributes, and is holy in His sight.   If this is so, it is a sin to deface the beauties of nature, and to make the world hideous in our haste to heap up money for ourselves. The insatiable greed of man has invaded the sanctuaries of unspoilt nature.   It has scoured the woods and the

mountains and the prairies and the lonely islets where the sea-birds make their habitations. Many beautiful species will be gone for ever in a few years unless the strong arm of the law puts a stop to the massacre.

122 It is for this country to take the lead in suppressing these outrages, which are a disgrace to civilisation, an offence against God, and a crime against posterity. Other nations, especially those in which the official teachers of religion and morals are the slaves of tradition, learning nothing and forgetting nothing, are sadly behindhand in this matter. With our wide Empire, we can do more than any other nation to protect animal life ; and we may be quite sure of this—that if our legislators will have the courage to deal firmly with this evil, disregarding the protests of a small number of interested persons, they will be considered by future ages to have taken a step forward in civilisation, and to have thereby brought honour to their country.

123 UTOPIAS

The Utopian is a poet who has gone astray.

124 Utopias are really the creation of the race-memory, which gives voice to deeper instincts than what we are in the habit of calling the lessons of history. It is an erroneous notion that we know a great deal about the past and nothing about the future. The things that we know about the past may be divided into those which probably never happened and those which do not much matter. As Samuel Butler says,

historians have the power, which is not claimed by the Deity, of altering the past; and this is perhaps the reason why they are allowed to exist. Historians, when they pretend to describe the past, are helping to make or mar the future. Utopias, on the other hand, are a revolt against modern trammels. Things are in the saddle and rule mankind. The horse wishes to fling up his heels now and then.

125 The making of Utopias is a masculine foible. I cannot recall any Utopia written by a woman; though most of them contain laws which women would resist either by the ancient method of a strike, as described by Aristophanes in the *Lysistrata*, or by the modern method of bombs. Most Utopias have been written by Englishmen or Frenchmen.

126 EUGENICS

If there is to be any improvement in human nature itself we must look to the infant science of eugenics to help us.

127 We are faced with a progressive deterioration of our stock, due to the suspension of natural selection, and the entire absence of anything like rational selection. The evil has been greatly increased by the stupidities of ignorant and unscientific class-legislation. We are threatened with something much worse than a regression to healthy barbarism. Let anyone contrast the physique of a Zulu or an Anatolian Turk with that of our slum population, and we shall realise

that we are breeding not vigorous barbarians but a new type of sub-men, abhorred by nature, and ugly as no natural product is ugly. We cannot find any comfort in the argument that this modification of environment at the expense of natural endowment is in the line of evolution, and therefore not only inevitable but beneficial. 'There is a way which seemeth right unto a man, but the ends thereof are the ways of death.' So-called progress, which is a rare episode in human history, has before now led a civilisation into a blind alley, from which there is no escape. Our tools have become our masters; to all appearance we work for them, and not they for us. They ought to be merely our instruments for realising a good and healthy life; they are in fact the means of our degeneration. Mechanism is morally neutral; it may be turned to good or to bad ends; and it is character only which decides whether it shall be well or badly used. A degenerate race cannot use its machinery to any good purpose. With its instinctive shrinking from intellectual effort, from exertion and from enterprise, it will concentrate its attention, as it is doing already, on labour-saving appliances to take the place of muscles and brains, till we shall soon have a generation which will call it a grievance to walk a mile, and which will think it the acme of civilisation to be able on every occasion to 'put a penny in the slot' in answer to the seductive advertisement, 'You press the button, we do the rest.' It has been proved a thousand times that nature takes away an organ which is not used. All our faculties were evolved during long ages in response to what were then our needs, by the stern but beneficent weeding of nature. In the absence of any systematic race-culture, we shall gradually slide back into feeble and helpless creatures, the destined prey of some more vigorous stock.

128 The best hope of stopping (this) progressive degeneration is in the science of eugenics. But this science is still too tentative to be made the basis of legislation, and we are not yet agreed what we should breed for. The two ideals, that of the perfect man and that of the perfectly organised State, would lead to very different principles of selection. Do we want a nation of beautiful and moderately efficient Greek gods, or do we want human mastiffs for policemen, human greyhounds for postmen, and so on? However, the opposition which eugenics has now to face is based on less respectable grounds, such as pure hedonism ('would the superman be any happier?'); indifference to the future welfare of the race ('posterity has done nothing for me; why should I do anything for posterity?'); and, in politics, the reflection that the unborn have no votes.

129 A good natural endowment, physical, mental, and moral, is more important, at any rate in these days, than an old coat-of-arms, or even than a fortune. An heiress is often the last survivor of a poor and dwindling stock. Galton was of the opinion that many able families have been extinguished by the 'taint of heiress blood.'

130   Much of our new philosophy is a kind of higher obscurantism; the man in the street applauds Bergson and William James because he dislikes science and logic, and values will, courage and sentiment.   He used to be fond of repeating that Waterloo was won on the playing fields of our public schools, until it was painfully obvious that Colenso and Spion Kop were lost in the same place.   We have muddled through so often that we have come to half-believe in a providence which watches over unintelligent virtue. ' Be good, sweet maid, and let who will be clever,' we have said to Britannia.   So we have acquiesced in being the worst educated people west of the Slav frontier.

131   Do we not see to-day the complex organisation of the ecclesiastic and college don succumbing before the simple squeezing and sucking apparatus of the profiteer and trade-unionist ?   If so-called civilised nations show any protracted vitality, it is because they are only civilised at the top.   Ancient civilisations were destroyed by imported barbarians ; we breed our own.

132   The students of eugenics are still exposed to ridicule and religious prejudice.   They have been pilloried in fiction as wishing to interfere with the right of every man and woman to please themselves in the choice of mates.   We have been invited to picture a state of society in which everybody is officially classified like the recruits in a conscript

army, and compelled to marry according to schedule.
Moralists have suspected them of wishing to introduce
the methods of a stud-farm. Socialists are indignant
at the suggestion that the pig sometimes makes the sty,
and not the sty the pig, and that even when all property
has been satisfactorily ' transferred ' (' Steal ? A fico
for the phrase ! " Convey " the wise it call,' says
Pistol, in Shakespeare), it may still be a problem how
to gather grapes of thorns and figs of thistles.

133   It is strange that Christians should be anti-eugenists.
For though religion is the strongest of *nurtural* influences,the religion of Christ, like eugenics, makes nature,
not nurture, its end. It aims at saving the soul—the
personality, the man himself—and in comparison with
this makes very light of his environment. A man is
saved, not by what he has, or knows, or even does, but
by what he is. Christianity treats all the apparatus of
life with a disdain as great as that of the biologist ; so
long as a man is inwardly healthy, it cares little whether
he is rich or poor, learned or simple. For the Christian
as for the eugenist, the test of the welfare of a country
is the quality of the men and women whom it turns
out. He cares nothing for the disparity between
births and deaths ; for him quality is everything,
quantity is nothing. And surely the Christian, who
is taught to fix his gaze on ' the Kingdom of God,'
and to pray that it may be set up on earth, is bound
to think of the welfare of posterity as a thing which
concerns him as much as that of his own generation.
And this welfare is conceived in terms of intrinsic

worth and healthiness. The Sermon on the Mount contains some admirable eugenic precepts, reminding us that a good tree cannot bring forth evil fruit, nor a corrupt tree good fruit. ' Do men gather grapes of thorns, or figs of thistles ? ' Christ may not have been thinking primarily of heredity, but He enunciates a universal law which applies to the family no less than to the individual.

134 PSYCHO-THERAPY

M. Charles Baudouin and M. Coué have given the public exactly what the public wants to believe. The civilised world is being devastated by an orgy of irrationalism. The intellect is useless—how pleasant to know this, when it is so much trouble to cultivate it ! The will is worse than useless ; for the more men will to cure a bad habit, the more often they fall into it. That is just what we have always found ; only stupid moralists have told us, ' If at first you don't succeed, try, try, try again.' And now we discover, with surprise and delight, that our guardian angel is the imagination, which surges up out of the deep pools of the subconscious, a mysterious but potent repository of all forgotten experiences and mental automatisms.

We are to train the subconscious, to coax it out of its hiding-places, to humbug it with soft words often repeated, until it flows over into our conscious life, submerging the stupid intellect and the interfering will ; and then we shall become happy and good and perfectly healthy.

135   This epidemic of irrationalism has given us pragmatism in philosophy, magic and superstition in religion, antinomianism in morals, post-impressionism in art, and Bolshevism in politics. At least, they all come from the father of lies, so I suppose they are closely related to each other, and I think I can see some relation between them. They all begin by saying: ' The true is what I choose to believe, and if I choose persistently enough I can make it so.'

136   Well, for my own part, I will have nothing to do with this world of make-believe.   It is an abomination to me.   I believe that my reason was given to me that I may know things as they are, and my will that I may bring my refractory disposition into harmony with the laws of my Creator. I will neither twist up the corners of my mouth when I am in the dumps, nor tell myself that in all respects I am getting better and younger and handsomer every day. If I can help it, I will play no tricks with my soul, in the faith that though bluff may sometimes pay very well in this world, it will cut a very poor figure in the next.

137 SCIENCE
       Of the teaching of science I am not competent to speak.   But as an instrument of mind-training, and even of liberal education, it seems to me to have a far higher value than is usually conceded to it by humanists. To direct the imagination to the infinitely great and the infinitely small, to vistas of time in which a thousand years are as one day ; to the

tremendous forces imprisoned in minute particles of matter; to the amazing complexity of the mechanism by which the organs of the human body perform their work; to analyse the light which has travelled for centuries from some distant star; to retrace the history of the earth and the evolution of its inhabitants—such studies cannot fail to elevate the mind, and only prejudice will disparage them. They promote also a fine respect for truth and fact, for order and outline, as the Greeks said, with a wholesome dislike of sophistry and rhetoric. The air which blows about scientific studies is like the air of a mountain top—thin, but pure and bracing.

138 In the natural sciences, England may claim the first place among the nations, and it is pleasant to observe that though in the other departments of intellectual activity there has been and is a dearth of very outstanding ability since the death of the great Victorians, there is no diminution in the output of first-rate work in physics and biology.

139 There is no sign whatever of the 'bankruptcy of science' which some of its enemies have been proclaiming. Its methods continue to work; they win new and signal triumphs every year; and can any thinker now be satisfied to cut the world of knowledge in two with a hatchet and to separate religion, ethics, and politics from the study of nature? It is not philosophers who are attracted by such a theory; it is politicians. They heap scorn on those whom they call 'intellectuals,' not because they are wrong, but

91

because they are few. They ignore the fact that they have to deal with Nature herself, who, as Plotinus says, is not in the habit of talking, but who is in the habit of striking.

140   It is a blunder to call scientific ethics ' materialistic.' The word is a mere term of abuse for anything that we do not like. If we believe in God, the laws of nature are the laws of God for the world in which we live. We know them only through the reason which God has given us; and it is that reason which finds law and order in the dance of atoms which is all that can be said to be presented to us from without. The laws of nature are a large part of Divine revelation. If we disregard them, and make, as Heracleitus said, a private world of our own, we shall not be ' splendid rebels,' but fools. And science is no friend either to selfishness or to hedonism. Self-sacrifice is part of nature's law.

141   The conception of Value enters far more deeply into purely scientific research than is commonly recognised. True reality as opposed to mere appearance is itself a value. That which ' only appears ' is not non-existent; it differs in value from what we call real existence, and what we call really existent depends largely on what we are interested in. Physicists tell us that the real nature of things is in the atoms, and that a table or chair is only a phenomenon. From this point of view, I suppose, a microbe is nearer reality than a man. That is because they choose to study nature from the point of view of the microbe.

They are radical pluralists. Some philosophers, beginning from the other end, have argued that ' the One remains, the many change and pass.' The distinction is psychological; it is a matter of interest or valuation. The historian, who also aspires to be scientific, studies the sequence of events with other values in his mind. Natural science confines itself to the logical value of generalisation; history studies those moral and social values which, though they transcend human lives, are actualised in human experience. Every kind of valuation rests on selection and abstraction. The faith in Order which makes natural science possible is only one example of a wider faith.

142 We are told that the scientific method is ultimately appropriate only to the abstractions of mathematics. But nature herself seems to have a taste for mathematical methods. A sane idealism believes that the eternal verities are adumbrated, not travestied, in the phenomenal world, and does not forget how much of what we call observation of nature is demonstrably the work of mind. The world as known to science is itself a spiritual world, from which certain valuations are, for special purposes, excluded.

143 The constructive task which lies before the next century is, if I may say so without presumption, to spiritualise science, as morality and art have already been spiritualised. The vision of God should appear to us as a triple star of truth, beauty, and goodness.

Wit and Wisdom

These are the three objects of all human aspirations ; and our hearts will never be at peace till all three alike rest in God.   Beauty is the chief mediator between the good and the true ; and this is why the great poets have been also prophets.   But Science at present lags behind ; she has not found her God ; and to this is largely due the ' unrest of the age.'   Much has already been done in the right direction by divines, philosophers, and physicists, and more still, perhaps, by the great poets, who have striven earnestly to see the spiritual background which lies behind the abstractions of materialistic science.   But much yet remains to be done.   We may agree with Hinton that ' Positivism bears a new Platonism in its bosom ' ; but the child has not yet come to the birth.

PART IV

LITERATURE

144 THE soul of England is reflected in our literature as much as in our history. We have borrowed styles and modes of writing as freely as the words which make up our language. Some of our greatest have borrowed most. But the national temper and spirit breathe from our literature as a whole, and by common consent some of our poets and prose writers have interpreted us to ourselves and to foreign nations with supreme fidelity.

145 We shall not recognise Shakespeare as the quintessential Englishman until we have learned to keep our encomiums of him ' on this side idolatry.' He had to wait for the Romantics before he fully came into his own ; they worshipped him, it must in time be owned, with too little discrimination. Perhaps he is, as we are accustomed to say, the greatest name in all literature ; but we cannot surrender to mankind the most typical of English dramatists. He has also been half buried under a talmud of commentary, over which no one would have laughed so heartily as himself.

146 It is to be hoped that we shall always have a few artists in words ; otherwise we shall soon have an

English language which will be as inferior to the English of the best writers as the Greek of Lucian is to the Greek of Plato. We have a glorious language, which, in the hands of Milton or Burke, is one of the grandest instruments of human speech; but, like everything else, it needs keeping in repair, especially in a hustling age when everyone reads and writes in a hurry.

147   Consider the wonderful variety of strong or beautiful English prose writing which the Victorian age produced. Froude, Macaulay, Newman, Ruskin, Pater, and Stevenson are each supreme in very different styles; and all of them achieved excellence by an amount of labour which very few writers are now willing to bestow.

148   An average Englishman is as little likely to take the poets for his spiritual guides as to wish that a philosopher was his king. Poets and philosophers are idealists; and, as a practical man, the average Englishman finds idealism out of place in so serious a business as saving his soul or governing the country. If he deigns to read the poets at all, they are the companions of his lightest or of his heaviest hours; he reads in bed after his morning tea, or devotes to the Muses the dregs of a busy day. We are not, as Carlyle complains, like the old Arabs, who would sing and kindle bonfires and solemnly thank the gods that in their tribe too a poet had shown himself. However that may be, the old Greeks, who are more important to us than

the old Arabs, used to sit at the feet of the poets, who were, as Aristophanes says, the schoolmasters of the full-grown. It is a pity that we do not treat our classics with the same seriousness. For the best of our English wisdom, and our clearest visions of the invisible, are enshrined in our poetry. Our best poetry is generally serious, moral, and often definitely religious in its aim.

149 THE VICTORIAN AGE

The grandest and most fully representative figure in all Victorian literature is Alfred Tennyson. And here let me digress for one minute. It was a good rule of Thomas Carlyle to set a portrait of the man whom he was describing in front of him on his writing-table. It is a practice which would greatly diminish the output of literary impertinence. Let those who are disposed to follow the present evil fashion of disparaging the great Victorians make a collection of their heads in photographs or engravings, and compare them with those of their own favourites. Let them set up in a row good portraits of Tennyson, Charles Darwin, Gladstone, Manning, Newman, Martineau, Lord Lawrence, Burne Jones, and, if they like, a dozen lesser luminaries, and ask themselves candidly whether men of this stature are any longer among us. I will not speculate on the causes which from time to time throw up a large number of great men in a single generation. I will only ask you to agree with me that since the golden age of Greece (assuming that we can trust the portrait busts of the

famous Greeks) no age can boast so many magnificent
types of the human countenance as the reign of Queen
Victoria. We, perhaps, being epigoni ourselves, are
more at home among our fellow-pygmies. Let us
agree with Ovid, if we will :

> Prisca iuvent alios ; ego me nunc denique natum
> Gratulor ; haec aetas moribus apta meis.

But let us have the decency to uncover before the
great men of the last century; and if we cannot
appreciate them, let us reflect that the fault may
possibly be in ourselves.

Tennyson's leonine head realises the ideal of a great
poet. And he reigned nearly as long as his royal
mistress. The longevity and unimpaired freshness of
the great Victorians has no parallel in history, except
in ancient Greece. The great Attic tragedians lived
as long as Tennyson and Browning; the Greek
philosophers reached as great ages as Victorian
theologians ; but if you look at the dates in other
flowering times of literature you will find that the life
of a man of genius is usually short, and his period of
production very short indeed.

150   Tennyson is now depreciated for several reasons.
His technique as a writer of verse was quite perfect;
our newest poets prefer to write verses which will not
even scan. He wrote beautifully about beautiful
things, and among beautiful things he included beautiful conduct. He thought it an ugly and disgraceful
thing for a wife to be unfaithful to her husband,

and condemned Guinevere and Lancelot as any sound moralist would condemn them. A generation which will not buy a novel unless it contains some scabrous story of adultery, and revels in the ' realism ' of the man with a muck-rake, naturally ' has no use for ' the ' Idylls of the King,' and calls Arthur the blameless prig.

151 There is no time to speak at length of the Victorian novel, another bright star in the firmament of the reign. Our nation has a great tradition in fiction, and we shall be wise to stick to it, instead of preferring a corrupt following of the French, whose novelists, in spite of their clever technique, seem to me frequently dull and usually repulsive. Dickens and Thackeray have been rivals, almost like Gladstone and Disraeli, and perhaps few are wholehearted admirers of both. That any educated reader should fail to love one or the other is to me inexplicable. The palmiest day of English novel-writing was in the fifties, when Dickens, Thackeray, Charlotte Brontë, George Eliot, Anthony Trollope, Kingsley, Disraeli, Bulwer Lytton, and Meredith were all writing. Later in the reign there was a short set-back, and the fortunes of English fiction seemed for a few years to be less promising than they became in the next generation, when several new writers of great ability and charm appeared. Now we seem to be once more in the trough of the wave ; and I cannot doubt that the main cause of the decay is the pernicious habit of writing hastily for money. If we take the trouble to consult Mr. Mudie's catalogue

of fiction, we shall learn to our amazement that there
are several writers, whose names we have never heard,
who have to their discredit over a hundred works of
fiction apiece. They obviously turn out several books
a year, just as a shoemaker manufactures so many pairs
of boots. The great novelists have generally written
rapidly, rather too rapidly; but such a cataract of
ink as these heroes of the circulating library spill is
absolutely inconsistent with even second-rate work.
Literature flourishes best when it is half a trade and
half an art; and here again the Victorian Age occupies
the most favourable part of the curve.

152   No country has had a more splendid succession of
inspiring teachers, whether poets, philosophers, or
men of letters. The idealistic tradition in England
is much older and more deeply rooted in the national
character than our temporary and partly accidental
addiction to material success. In proportion as our
people can be taught to interest themselves in those
treasures of the soul, in which one man's gain is not
another man's loss, and which are increased by being
shared with others, we may hope that the bitterness
and narrowness of economic strife may be assuaged,
and that something like a really harmonious civilisation
may come in sight.

PART V

ENGLAND

153 I TAKE up my parable as a man who is proud to be
a pure Englishman, with no admixture of Scottish,
Irish, Welsh or other blood for at least three hundred
years, before which date my family does not seem to
have been recognised by the College of Heralds.
Judging by my patronymic, I suppose my ancestor
'came over' as a Scandinavian pirate, and was,
I dare say, as great a ruffian as most of William the
Conqueror's Normans; but history is silent. 'In
spite of all temptations to belong to other nations,'
I am glad to be an Englishman pure and simple.

154 There is no limit to the noble aspirations which the
words ' my country ' may evoke.

155 What Britain stands for is what Britain is. We
have long known in our hearts what Britain stands
for; but we have now been driven to search our
thoughts and make our ideals explicit to ourselves and
others. The Englishman has become a philosopher
malgré lui. 'Whatever the world thinks,' writes
Bishop Berkeley, ' he who hath not much meditated
upon God, the human soul, and the *summum bonum*,

101

may possibly make a thriving earthworm, but will most indubitably make a sorry patriot and a sorry statesman.' These words, which were quoted by Mr. Arthur Balfour a few years ago, may seem to make a large demand on the average citizen; but in our quiet way we have all been meditating on these things since last August (1914), and we know pretty well what our *summum bonum* is for our country.

We believe in chivalry and fair play and kindliness —these things first and foremost; and we believe, if not exactly in democracy, yet in a government under which a man may think and speak the thing he wills. We do not believe in war, and we do not believe in bullying, we do not flatter ourselves that we are the supermen; but we are convinced that the ideas which we stand for, and which we have on the whole tried to carry out, are essential to the peaceful progress and happiness of humanity; and for these ideas we have drawn the sword. The great words of Abraham Lincoln have been on the lips of many and in the hearts of all since the beginning of the great contest : ' With malice towards none; with charity for all; with firmness in the right as God gives us to see the right— let us strive on to finish the work we are in.'

156   What a long list of great achievements this one-sided civilisation has to its credit ! It broke Napoleon, whose power was exhausted by the invincible spirit of the ruling oligarchy, by the dogged patriotism of the people generally, and by the immense productivity of the English factories. It was still strong enough

to wear out the Germans in the Great War. It spread the English language and institutions over the whole world, and brought one quarter of the globe, and of its population, under the flag of order and liberty. It brought cheap comforts within the reach of nearly the whole people, for the first time in history. Never before has modest comfort been so widely diffused.

157 There must be many thousands of Englishmen who, like myself, were awake all night after the first ominous bulletin about Jutland, which seemed to hint at a great naval disaster. But all through the war, when things were looking bad, I tried to remember another scene from English history. We are told that in the days of the Commonwealth Bulstrode Whitelocke, Ambassador to The Hague, was tossing about through the night in anxiety about the condition of his country. An old servant, lying in the same room, addressed him : ' Sir, may I ask you a question ? ' ' Certainly,' replied the Ambassador. ' Sir, did God govern the world well before you came into it ? ' ' Undoubtedly.' ' And will He rule the world well when you have gone out of it ? ' ' Undoubtedly.' ' Then, sir, can you not trust Him to rule the world well while you are in it ? ' The tired Ambassador turned on his side and fell asleep.

158 We have no wish to boast of ' England's effort ' (for the War) ; it is better to leave our actions to the impartial verdict of history. That verdict will, I believe, be that no more extraordinary exhibition

of energy and resolution has ever been recorded than that by which an unmilitary nation, quite unprepared for war, mobilised over nine million of men, financed its allies, supplied them with munitions, and policed the high seas.

159 The habit of blaming and criticising our own country is ingrained among Englishmen, and when it is practised by sincere patriots it does good. The British lion always rouses himself to fresh efforts by lashing himself with his tail. But undoubtedly it encourages our enemies to defame us, when they hear us accusing ourselves. And unfortunately it also encourages the noxious breed of domestic traitors, the friends of their country's enemies for the time being, who whenever England is in difficulties try to make out that their country is in the wrong. Whether we are contending against white, black or brown antagonists, these disinterested friends of the human race (except England) come forward with their advocacy of the other side. We differ, it would seem, from all other misguided persons by never being in the right, even by accident. But it will generally be found that the anti-English Englishman has alien blood in his veins.

160 It may well be that now that our mission as a world power is nearly accomplished—for we may hope that the young Englands beyond the seas will soon be strong enough to protect themselves—we may realise another and not less worthy ambition, that of being

the spiritual home and ancestral hearth of a number
of vigorous nations, speaking our language and moulded
on our traditions. Whether this will be so will depend
on the temper in which we meet the trials of the next
fifty years. Are we ready to welcome a new out-
pouring of the spirit, if such should be granted us?
An Englishman who loves his country will hope, but
not without many misgivings. We are being rocked
on a turbid stream, and it is not easy to feel sure
whether the current is bearing us to weal or woe.
Just now the populace is seen at its worst; it is waxing
fat and kicking; but adversity may bring out a better
side, as we found when our prospects in the war
looked black. I am no optimist; but I cling to the
faith of Wordsworth's sonnet, composed when we
were at death-grips with Bonaparte:

> It is not to be thought of that the Flood
> Of British freedom, which, to the open sea
> Of the world's praise, from dark antiquity
> Hath flowed, ' with pomp of waters, unwithstood,'
> Roused though it be full often to a mood
> Which spurns the check of salutary bands,
> That this most famous Stream in bogs and sands
> Should perish, and to evil and to good
> Be lost for ever.

161   It may well be that the historian of the future will
name the year of the Second Jubilee of Queen Victoria,
or the end of the nineteenth century, or the death of
the old Queen, as the culminating point of England

as a world-power. Since then, the colossus has tottered. It has been a bad sign that England, in the narrower sense, has not taken her proper place as the predominant partner. We are governed by Scots, Welsh, Irish, and Jews. At the Armistice after the Great War, we were represented by Lloyd George, Bonar Law, Lord Reading, Balfour, Geddes, Haig, Wemyss, and Milner. The genuinely English patriotism of Kipling and Henley is resented. We are no longer Englishmen ; we are ' Britons.' There has been a proposal to alter the name of the Calcutta ' Englishman ' ; it was not, needless to say, the natives who objected to the title. It is a small thing ; but it seems to indicate a loss of confidence in ourselves and our destiny.

162   In every department of life the place of the Victorian giants is filled (it seems to me) by pygmies. As in the days of Eli, the word of the Lord is precious— there is no open vision. This state of things will pass ; we shall have great men again before long ; and they will have to address themselves to the great problem which is at the bottom of all lesser departmental problems—the desire of the progressive nations of the North and West to beat out for themselves a really native civilisation, which hitherto they have never enjoyed. We are still the barbarians who broke up the Roman Empire and took over what we could lift of its culture. Our religious books come from Palestine ; our ' humaner letters ' from Athens and

Rome; our whole mental furniture, except our science, is a queer assortment of miscellaneous antiques, which we wear as incongruously as an African chief decks himself in European clothes. And beneath all there is our own native moral ideal, our secular religion which we have evolved for ourselves, which we believe in and live by—the Northern European code of honour—the ideal of a gentleman. It is a queer state of things, and we shall not see our way out till we have more genius among us than can at present be discerned.

163   I have no doubt that the Elizabethan and the Victorian Ages will appear to the historian of the near future as the twin peaks in which English civilisation culminated. There may be a third, equally splendid, period yet to come, but I do not think that any of us will live to see it. The remainder of the twentieth century will be handicapped by the necessity of clearing up the mess made in the last eight years. However, the Napoleonic War was followed, as I have argued, by a very great age, and I will not be so rash as to prophesy what England will be like thirty years hence. It is for you, my younger readers, to answer that question, for the answer depends on yourselves. We old Victorians will before then have made room for you by quitting a world to which, as I am sure you think, we no longer belong.

164   In plain living and high thinking will be our salvation, or the salvation of the 'remnant' which will survive the turmoils of an age of transition.

Plain living will be forced upon us, whether we will or not, for the conditions of prosperity are in part slipping from us, and in part are being wantonly thrown away ; high thinking will not only make us citizens of the City ' whose type is laid up in heaven,' but will mitigate the acerbities of a struggle for which the responsibility cannot be laid solely on the shoulders of any one class. Aristotle would teach us that ' to be always seeking after utilities does not become free and elevated souls,' and that ' we must train the nobler sort of natures not to desire more than they have got.' But the New Testament is equally insistent that whatever work we have to do must be done ' heartily, as to the Lord and not to men,' and that those who will not work have no claim on the community for maintenance. Still more decisive is the warning that a house divided against itself cannot stand.

165 I lay down my pen with the consciousness that I have not painted a bright picture of the near future of my country. It is quite true that, in my opinion, the waters which we have now to navigate are likely to be stormy, and that the anti-social ferments within the nation are unusually malignant. But just as a healthy body generates anti-toxins to combat any virulent infection, so our nation may be vigorous enough to neutralise the poisons which now threaten our civilisation with death. Nothing but good can be done by calling attention to perils which really exist, and which may easily escape due attention amid the bottomless insincerity of modern politics and political journalism.

166   I have laid bare my hopes and fears for the country that I love. This much I can avow, that never, even when the storm-clouds appear blackest, have I been tempted to wish that I was other than an Englishman.

167 THE KING

There is much to be said for our present system of making the King the head of the social organisation of the country, with only nominal political power. Our King receives much of the loyalty and devotion which Americans pay to their flag. The Throne is the least criticised and apparently the most stable of all our institutions ; and if its occupant is just a good specimen of an English gentleman, that is what most of his subjects wish him to be. We have seen enough of clever sovereigns abroad ; perhaps we have had enough of clever prime ministers at home.

168 THE HOUSE OF COMMONS

The House of Commons has been saved repeatedly by the traditional sense of its greatness and venerability, which has given the political career a greater prestige in England than in any other country. But this prestige has been much impaired, as we can see by the change in the daily Press. The British householder fifty years ago used to read the parliamentary debates through with reverent care every morning ; they were presented as the most important part of the paper. Now the Press is a variety entertainment, and politics are at best one turn among many others.

The debates are not fully reported, and nobody would read them if they were. We are losing faith in government by debate, especially now that the debates are unreal. And the payment of members does not seem to have made politicians more independent, but rather less so.

169   The House of Commons as a whole is a very capable body of men, with wholesomely diversified antecedents and attainments. If they were united, as the members of parliament in Queen Victoria's reign were united (with the exception of the Irish) in a desire to use their trust, as Burke says, in the interest of ' the whole,' they would be as efficient a body of legislators as we could reasonably hope to obtain by any other method of choice. But the whole system is threatened with ruin by the increasing prevalence and power of sectionalism. Any large and organised body, which recognises no duties to the State as a whole, but only to one class, may make popular government impossible. We have seen already how parliament is paralysed by the anti-social or anti-patriotic action of some violent clique. The members of these cliques in parliament are not free agents ; they have pledged their votes beforehand. This reduces debate to a farce ; speeches are not made to convince their hearers, but either to be read in the newspapers, or to obstruct the progress of government legislation. Attendance at debates is more and more felt to be waste of time, and the reputation of parliament in the country declines.

PART VI

REFLECTIONS

170 ON WISDOM

Recognition by others is essential to all but the strongest and proudest virtue. I think I should put it third among the gifts which I should ask from the fairy godmother. I should wish first for wisdom, like King Solomon ; and by wisdom I mean a just estimate of the relative values of things. My second wish would be for domestic happiness, and my third for the approval of my fellows.

171 Let none of us delude himself by supposing that honesty is always the best policy. It is not. It is ridiculous to deny that a man whose whole energies are bent upon his own advancement, is more likely to secure his end than the man who seeks first the kingdom of God and His righteousness. The world belongs to those who think and act with it, who keep a finger on its pulse. The way to be successful is to give the public exactly what it wants, and about ten per cent. more of it than it expects. It is indeed astonishing with how little wisdom mankind can be governed, when that little wisdom is their own.

172 Unworldliness based on knowledge of the world is the finest thing on earth ; but unworldliness based on ignorance of the world is less admirable.

173 The wisdom of the wise is an uncommon degree of common sense.

174 We cannot afford to throw away the wisdom of the past. It is too precious a treasure to be lost.

175 The problem of the reformer is complicated by the fact that we must accept the heavy burdens of the past.

176 There is no greater disloyalty to the great pioneers of human progress than to refuse to budge an inch from where they stood.

177 The wisest man can only achieve an application of the living past to the living present.

178 Diagnosis is not the same as cure; but in some diseases it is more than half of the physician's task.

179 There are of course no beginnings or ends in history. We may walk for a few miles by the side of a river, noting its shallows and its rapids, the gorges which confine it and the plains through which it meanders; but we know that we have seen neither the beginning nor the end of its course, that the whole river has an unbroken continuity, and that sections, whether of space or time, are purely arbitrary. We are always sowing our future; we are always reaping our past. The Industrial Revolution began in reality before the accession of George III, and the French monarchy was stricken with mortal disease before Louis XV bequeathed his kingdom to his luckless successor.

On the Future

180   Mankind has honoured its destroyers and persecuted its benefactors, building palaces for living brigands, and tombs for long-dead prophets.

181   We have forgotten that hitherto the nations which have put mankind and posterity most in their debt have been small States—Israel, Athens, Florence, Elizabethan England.

182   Many of our discontents are externalised soul-aches. By brooding over them we hurt our Souls and immerse them in 'Matter.' A restoration of internal and external peace is possible only when we rise to the vision of the real, the spiritual world.

183 ON THE FUTURE
      In the time of decay and disintegration which lies before us, more persons will seek consolation where it can be found.

184   We shall need 'a remnant' to save Europe from relapsing into barbarism; for the new forces are almost wholly cut off from the precious traditions which link our civilisation with the great eras of the past. The possibility of another dark age is not remote; but there must be enough who value our best traditions to preserve them till the next spring-time of civilisation. We must take long views, and think of our great-grandchildren.

185   I have, I suppose, made it clear that I do not consider myself specially fortunate in having been born in

1860, and that I look forward with great anxiety to
the journey through life which my children will have
to make. But, after all, we judge our generation
mainly by its surface currents. There may be in
progress a storage of beneficent forces which we cannot see. There are ages of sowing and ages of
reaping : the brilliant epochs may be those in which
spiritual wealth is squandered, the epochs of apparent
decline may be those in which the race is recuperating
after an exhausting effort. To all appearance, man
has still a great part of his long lease before him, and
there is no reason to suppose that the future will be less
productive of moral and spiritual triumphs than the
past. The source of all good is like an inexhaustible
river ; the Creator pours forth new treasures of goodness, truth, and beauty for all who will love them and
take them. ' Nothing that truly *is* can ever perish,'
as Plotinus says : whatever has value in God's sight
is safe for evermore. Our half-real world is the factory
of souls, in which we are tried, as in a furnace. We
are not to set our hopes upon it, but to learn such
wisdom as it can teach us while we pass through it.

186   I think there is some danger that another eclipse
of culture may come upon us. The continuity of the
present with the past is in some danger of being lost.
A generation is growing up, not uneducated, but
educated in a system which neglects the historical
development of European civilisation. The classics
are not taught ; and the Bible, which has been a great
popular educator in England, is no longer much read.

On Wastefulness

187   The East has much to teach the West, and perhaps
we may be willing to learn, now that the West is
uneasily conscious that the civilisation of the East may
menace our own, and perhaps outlast it.   The Indian
and Chinese peasant, with his frugal wants, based on
immemorial tradition, may have a greater survival
value than the American artisan with his £1000 a year,
his Ford car, his bejewelled wife, and his daily visit
to the ' movies.'

188   Prophecy is only an amusement ; what does concern
us all deeply is that we should see in what direction we
are now moving.

189   When we consider the achievements of any nation
which even for fifty years has grasped a fringe of the
mantle of God, we shall not think that Christ, or
Plato, is bidding us to lose substance for shadow.   The
Soul of the race mocks at the triumphs of Sennacherib
and Attila.   They, and Cleon, are only remembered
because their victims have thought it worth while to
hold them up to infamy.   Human societies are happy
in proportion as they have their treasure in that class
of goods which are not lessened by being shared.

190   The ascent of the soul to God, which is made by
thousands in the short span of a single life, may be
an earnest of what humanity shall one day achieve.

191 ON WASTEFULNESS
The extreme wastefulness of modern civilisation
ought to alarm us.   We are recklessly using up the

natural resources of the planet, as well as defacing its beauty beyond repair. Civilisation is becoming more and more artificial, and therefore more and more precarious. 'There is a way which seemeth right unto a man, but the ends thereof are the ways of death.'

192　Simplicity redeems from waste not only money but time, some of our own and more of other people's. It is not a comfortable thought that we often use up the product of a long day's work in an hour, and on something which does us no real good at all.

193　The real gravamen against the owner of wealth is that he often spends his money in a vulgar, tasteless, and unpatriotic manner. The way of living adopted by many of the new rich is as morally objectionable as it is politically insane. It is no new thing that 'beggars on horseback ride their horse to death'; the cause is not so much ethical callousness as gross ignorance of the art of living. The working man, if his wages are suddenly doubled, behaves in the same way. There is no point in which we are so inferior to France as in the art of spending. The remedy is partly moral, but must be sought mainly in a better education.

194　It may be doubted whether nature intended the Englishman to be a money-making animal.

195　Civilisation is being poisoned by its own waste products, by the rotten human material that we protect and foster so carefully.

196 ON SENTIMENTALISM

Unfortunately, experience shows that none is so cruel as the disillusioned sentimentalist. He thinks that he can break or ignore nature's laws with impunity ; and then, when he finds that nature has no sentiment, he rages like a mad dog, and combines with his theoretical objection to capital punishment a lust to murder all who disagree with him. This is the genesis of Jacobinism and Bolshevism.

197 The so-called conflict between the head and the heart is generally a conflict between reflective and unreflective thought, or between reason and prejudice. 'The heart' is a popular judge, because it decides in favour of the defendant without hearing the prosecution.

198 The fruit of the tree of knowledge always drives man from some paradise or other ; and even the paradise of fools is not an unpleasant abode while it is habitable.

199 As a rule, the game of life is worth playing, but the struggle is the prize.

200 ON PARTY LABELS

The Christian graces care nothing for names and labels ; where the Spirit of the Lord is, there they abide, but not in great Churches that have forgotten Him. How little of Joy there is in the character of the religious bigot or fanatic, or in the prudent ecclesiastical statesman ! A show of cheerfulness they may cultivate, as they often do; but it is like the crackling of thorns under a pot: we cannot mistake it for the joy of the Lord which is the strength of the true Christian.

201   It is becoming impossible for those who mix at all with their fellow-men to believe that the grace of God is distributed denominationally.

202   If the devil invented partisan labels—and I think he must have done so—it was one of the cleverest tricks he ever played.

203 ON LETTER WRITING

We must hope, without much confidence, that the graceful and gentle art of letter-writing may have another flowering time among us.

204   We have often been told that the penny post killed real letter-writing. But the two-penny post does not seem to have improved the quality or to have seriously diminished the quantity of letters which are certainly not literature.

205   As an example of the short letter—a masterpiece —a father told his son at school that he was too busy to read long letters, and requested the boy to be brief. The answer was a model of terseness: ' S.O.S., L.S.D., R.S.V.P.'

206   A Royal duke is said to have written to an Irish bishop: ' Dear Cork, Please ordain Stanhope. Yours, York '; to which the reply was : ' Dear York, Stanhope's ordained. Yours, Cork.'

207   Worse than the telephone and the postcard is the pose of being overworked. We do not really get through more sound work than our grandfathers; but we make a conscience of being always in a hurry—unless, indeed, we are trade unionists, with whom the charge of hurrying is a deadly reproach. We can travel much faster than our grandfathers, and accordingly, we waste much more time in going from place to place. Time-saving inventions have much to answer for in shortening our leisure.

208   ON BOOKS AND WRITERS
    Of course, we do not as a rule read the books of pioneers, who by inspiring their successors have helped to put themselves out of date.

209   As a rule the modern author does not give himself time; he is in too great a hurry to make money, for good writing is desperately slow work. Poets generally write good prose, because they are accustomed to slow composition.

210   Leslie Stephen wanted everyone to leave his autobiography tied up with his will. I am afraid most of us would find the compilation rather embarrassing.

211   Reminiscences are not the perfect autobiography. The present modifies the past by interpreting it. We want the text without the commentary. How did his life appear to the great man before he knew that he was great?

212   If, however, a man writes a diary which he feels sure that nobody will ever see except himself, he is

probably perfectly truthful. There is no motive for being otherwise. He is no more ashamed of recording his actions, good and bad, just as they happened, than of seeing himself in his bath.

213 ON AMERICANS

An American citizen, a prohibitionist on strike, fell on his face in the gutter. Rising to his feet, he wiped his hands on the nearest object resembling a towel, which happened to be the Stars and Stripes hanging out of a shop window. Another American citizen came by and knocked him down. He did this not because he cared for ' Old Glory,' but because he also was drunk and wanted to fight. He was arrested by a policeman and brought before a magistrate on a charge of assault and battery. While awaiting the proceedings, he bethought himself of pleading that he had acted hastily, because his patriotic feelings were excited by an outrage on the National Flag. The magistrate not only dismissed the case, but requested the honour of shaking hands with such a model citizen. The newspapers took the matter up, and thousands of pounds were subscribed to buy a suitable residence for the noble fellow.

Now if this had happened in England, say at Ascot, and the tipsy man had wiped his fingers on the coat of King Edward, there is not the slightest doubt what His Majesty would have said, but there the incident would probably have ended. If a bystander had knocked the man down, he would presumably have been fined five shillings, and certainly nobody would have bought him a house.

On Americans

Why do our cousins treat a piece of bunting as a religious emblem and think it an antiquated prejudice to feel reverence for a human being who represents the nation ? Homage to a flag or a mace seems to be a half-way house between loyalty to the person of the chief magistrate and no loyalty at all, which is the consistent attitude of the Socialists, who snort at the Union Jack.

214   The ties which bind the two nations (America and England) together—our common language, literature, and institutions—must in the long run prove far stronger than the temporary and almost accidental causes of estrangement—the dim memories of the War of Independence, the very unfair schoolbooks from which American children learn their history, and the malice of certain immigrants and their descendants, who must in time be absorbed in the mass of American nationals, and drop their senseless inherited vendettas.

215   We picture the typical American, healthy, clean-minded, and indomitably cheerful, springing from his bed in the morning, and, after a bath and deep-breathing exercises, to which he attaches great importance, praying that in the coming day he may be helpful to others, happy, strenuous, and successful. He asks himself no difficult questions ; the proof of his religion is that it makes him a very efficient member of society. This kind of Christianity is so utterly unlike Catholicism that we may wonder what an American does when he joins the Church of Rome.

But he is not at all embarrassed ; he belongs to the biggest religion on earth, anyway ; and America has three Cardinals.

216   Democracy—the magic ballot-box—has few worshippers any longer except in America, where men will still shout for about two hours—and indeed much longer—that she is ' great.'

217   The fact is that the Americans are not a thoughtful people ; they are too busy to stop and question their values.

218 ON THE JEWS
    We think that every country gets the Jews that it deserves ; and that we, who treat our Jewish fellow-citizens with decency, have both deserved and got the best Jews.

219   Above all other nations, we English accept a man for what he is worth, and do not penalise him because he is an immigrant.   The result is, as I said, that the English are the only really down-trodden race in Europe.   We have a Welsh Prime Minister, two Scotch archbishops, and any number of Jews, Scots, and Irish in prominent places.   But by so doing we are better served, and we have enriched our stock by blending it with desirable foreigners of all sorts.

220   I once heard a dignified clergyman say pompously : ' We owe the Jews more than we can ever repay.' To which I felt inclined to answer : ' I hope, sir, that in your case it is only a temporary embarrassment.'

On Home and Happiness

221   Race-consciousness is a rather silly thing. The sensible man takes his neighbours as he finds them, and is not too ready to believe in dark conspiracies.

222   ON HOME AND HAPPINESS
The word ' home ' is associated with all that makes life beautiful and sacred, with tender memories of joy and sorrow, and especially with the first eager outlook of the young mind upon a wonderful world. A man does not as a rule feel much sentiment about his London house, still less about his office or factory. It is for the home of his childhood, or of his ancestors, that a man will fight most readily, because he is bound to it by a spiritual and poetic tie.

223   On the whole, the happiest people seem to be those who have no particular cause for being happy except the fact that they are so—a good reason, no doubt. And yet I should not choose a naturally contented temperament as my first request from a fairy godmother. It would be unfortunate if I said, ' I wish to be the happiest man in England,' and promptly found myself locked up in an asylum, a cheerful lunatic who believed himself to be the Emperor of China. For all we know to the contrary, the happiest man in England may be a madman, and none of us would wish to change places with him. And even if the always cheerful person is perfectly sane, he is without the ' splendid spur ' which most men need if they are to do much with their lives.

224 ON THE WORLD AND OURSELVES

The world which, as we think, surrounds us, the world of which we are conscious, is made up of the things we care about, the things which we choose to attend to. All the rest slips away from us unperceived. To the actor, all the world's a stage ; to the pushing, ambitious man it is a *mêlée* in which methods of barbarism, slightly disguised, pay best ; to the servant of Mammon it is a counting-house or a field to be exploited. To the spiritual man it is the forecourt of God's house, and he knows at all times where to find the Master.

225   The world as it is, is the world as God sees it, not as we see it. Our vision is distorted, not so much by the limitations of finitude, as by sin and ignorance. The more we can raise ourselves in the scale of being, the more will our ideas about God and the world correspond to the reality.

226   The worst shadows that hide the Sun from us are those which we make ourselves by standing in our own light, by putting the swollen and lumpish image of the false self between the hidden man of the heart and his God.

227   I think we can generally see some reason in our own troubles, not perhaps when they first fall upon us, but in retrospect ; it is the apparent injustice and irrationality of fate in its dealings with others which sometimes oppresses us.

228   The Stoics used to say that the selfish"man is a cancer in the universe. A cancer is caused by unchecked proliferation of cellular tissue by one organ independently of the rest of the body. The parallel is therefore scientifically exact.

229   All we have a right to say is that individuals are occasionally guided by reason, crowds never.

230   We really know very little about the people whom we meet. We see their faces, which are not much more than masks, but we cannot read their hearts. Robert Browning thanks God that the meanest of his creatures has two soul-sides, one to face the world with, one to show a woman when he loves her. It is only in the intimacy of family life, or in that rare thing, a perfect friendship, that the veil is partially drawn aside. And even then we do not lay bare our hearts entirely.

231   Ask yourselves, Who are the people who have really helped me ? You will find, I think, that they have been laymen more often than clergymen, women perhaps more often than men ; that the occasions have been most trivial, that the words spoken and things done have been slight and unpremeditated. They have been sidelights upon the person's character, peeps into the inner life of one whom God hides privily by His own presence from the provoking of all men ; whose mind is kept in perfect peace because it is stayed on God ; of one who sees God because his heart is pure. It is the sudden sting of self-reproach.

the shame of the contrast, the longing to be like such an one, to see things as he sees them, that sticks in a man's mind, and sends him to his knees as soon as he is alone. Sometimes when such a man or woman dies, we learn for the first time, not without surprise, what he or she has been to many. Such persons have laid up a rich store of gratitude by being what God has helped them to be. A character can never be refuted or ignored; disinterestedness is always interesting.

232 The true apostolical succession, in the lives of the saints, has never failed, and never will.

233 We are justified in believing that the world as God sees it is far more beautiful and harmonious than the world as we see it. But then we assume that the defect is in us, not in the world, and we do not suppose either that if we were reborn as we are now ten thousand years hence, we should find everything better, or that we can live in a world of fancy which has no roots in experience.

234 It is God, and not the speaker, who can make the poor sounds of the human voice the vehicles of grace, and it is the sincere word, not the clever one, which is most likely to be thus honoured.

235 I have never understood why it should be considered derogatory to the Creator to suppose that He has a sense of humour. The lack of this sense is considered a defect in human nature; and some of us would think that heaven would be very dull without

it.   The world is full of absurdities which to a superior Being may afford infinite merriment.   Several animals are laughable, though few are really ugly ; and many of the antics of our own species must seem exquisitely ridiculous to anyone observing them from outside. We often, without meaning it, picture God as a sour Puritan.   It would be easier to justify His ways to man if we pictured Him more genially.

236   What we are matters much more than what we do or say.   At the core of every man's soul, deeper even than consciousness, lies the hidden man of the heart who can hear God speak.   And if in ourselves that inmost shrine is a temple of the Holy Ghost, our words and actions will show from whence they came. Deep calleth unto deep ; and those whose hearts God has touched can find their way easily to the hearts of others.   The soul may have wandered far from its true home ; but when it meets one who has *been there*, who can bring it tidings of that dear and half-forgotten land, it will spring to meet him.   Here is someone who knows ; he can tell me what I want to know.

237   Love and suffering cut the deepest channels in our souls, and reveal the most precious of God's secrets. Even in national life we can see that the characteristic utterances of ages of prosperity—the Augustan Ages of history—are less penetrating and of less universal significance than those which have been wrung from nations in agony.

238   The fact of suffering is not an evil but a good, since it is the chief means of progress, of which it implies the possibility.   A common error in our day is horror at the symptoms and neglect of the disease.

239   A horror of sin is at the root of every vigorous religious creed. The opposition of good and evil, which from the moral standpoint is radical and irreducible, must be fully recognised in religion, unless religion is to be sublimated into a theosophy, or degraded into ritual, cultus and magic.

240   Admission to redemptive work, which is the sign and fruit of redemption, is the reward of complete self-consecration.

241   And we too, in our hope for ourselves, our families, and our dear country, must be content to commit ourselves into God's hands in Faith. The future is hidden from us, mercifully perhaps. It may not bring what we most wish for. Our hopes may have to be transmuted like the Messianic hopes of the first Christians.

242   I believe from the bottom of my heart that our spiritual life in all its stages is informed and guided by the objectively real presence of Christ within us, by an actual continuation of the work which was begun when He was visibly present among His disciples in Galilee.

LIST OF REFERENCES

TITLES OF BOOKS QUOTED

'The Philosophy of Plotinus.'   2 vols.
'Christian Mysticism.'
'Outspoken Essays.'   2 vols.
'England.'
'Personal Idealism and Mysticism.'
'Personal Religion and the Life of Devotion.'
'The Platonic Tradition in English Religious Thought.'
'Speculum Animae.'
'Types of Christian Saintliness.'
'The Church and the Age.'
'Science and Ultimate Truth.'
'Lay Thoughts of a Dean.'
'Cambridge Essays on Education.'

The running numbers refer to the paragraphs in the text.

1 'Outspoken Essays,' II. 1
2 'Outspoken Essays,' II. 55
3 'Speculum Animae,' 42
4 'The Platonic Tradition,' 27–29
5 'Personal Religion,' 20, 21
6 'Plotinus,' I. 5
7 'Personal Religion,' 18
8 'Lay Thoughts,' 327
9 'Personal Religion,' 27–28
10 'Personal Religion,' 32
11 'Personal Religion,' 31
12 'Outspoken Essays,' II. 14
13 'Outspoken Essays,' II. 15
14 'Christian Mysticism,' 329–330
15 'Outspoken Essays,' II. 15, 16
16 'Speculum Animae, 12–13
17 'Speculum Animae,' 47
18 'Plotinus,' II. 201–202
19 'Speculum Animae,' 19–20
20 'Outspoken Essays, II, 49
21 'Speculum Animae,' 20
22 'Personal Idealism,' 87–88
23 'Speculum Animae,' 22–23

List of References

List of References

78 'Personal Religion,' 73
79 'Personal Religion, 73–74
80 'Personal Religion,' 74
81 'Personal Idealism,' 105
82 'Outspoken Essays,' II. 148–149
83 'Outspoken Essays,' II. 180
84 'Outspoken Essays,' II. 230
85 'Outspoken Essays,' II. 228
86 'Outspoken Essays,' II. 173–4
87 'The Platonic Tradition,' 109–110
88 'Plotinus,' II. 223
89 'Outspoken Essays,' II. 169–170
90 'Outspoken Essays,' II. 183
91 'The Platonic Tradition,' 107
92 'Outspoken Essays,' I. 20–21
93 'England,' 273
94 'Speculum Animae,' 3–4
95 'England,' 188
96 'Outspoken Essays,' I. 98–99
97 'England,' 212–213
98 'Lay Thoughts,' 49
99 'Outspoken Essays,' I. 7
100 'Outspoken Essays,' I. 8
101 'Outspoken Essays,' I. 9–10
102 'Outspoken Essays,' I. 11
103 'Outspoken Essays,' I. 12

104 'Outspoken Essays,' II. 85–86
105 'Outspoken Essays,' I. 28–29
106 'Outspoken Essays,' I. 41–42
107 'Outspoken Essays,' I. 56–57
108 'Plotinus,' II. 224
109 'Lay Thoughts,' 220–221
110 'Lay Thoughts,' 221–222
111 'Lay Thoughts,' 217–218
112 'England,' 55–56
113 'England,' 55
114 'Lay Thoughts,' 262
115 'Lay Thoughts,' 263
116 'Lay Thoughts,' 263
117 'Lay Thoughts,' 197
118 'Lay Thoughts,' 198
119 'Lay Thoughts,' 199
120 'Lay Thoughts,' 200
121 'Lay Thoughts,' 200–201
122 'Lay Thoughts,' 201
123 'Lay Thoughts,' 202
124 'Lay Thoughts,' 203
125 'Lay Thoughts,' 203–204
126 'Outspoken Essays,' I. 25
127 'Outspoken Essays,' II. 266–267
128 'Outspoken Essays,' II. 175
129 'Lay Thoughts,' 249
130 'Cambridge Essays,' 14
131 'Outspoken Essays,' II. 166
132 'Lay Thoughts,' 244
133 'Outspoken Essays,' II. 273–274

List of References

134 'Lay Thoughts,' 230–231
135 'Lay Thoughts,' 232
136 'Lay Thoughts,' 236
137 'Cambridge Essays,' 23–24
138 'England,' 80
139 'Outspoken Essays,' II. 146
140 'Outspoken Essays,' II. 147
141 'Science and Ultimate Truth,' 8–9
142 'Cambridge Essays,' 21
143 'Christian Mysticism,' 322
144 'England,' 82
145 'England,' 83
146 'Lay Thoughts,' 84
147 'Outspoken Essays,' II. 206
148 'The Platonic Tradition,' 66–67
149 'Outspoken Essays,' II. 199–200
150 'Outspoken Essays,' II. 200–201
151 'Outspoken Essays,' II. 205
152 'England,' 289
153 'Lay Thoughts,' 165
154 'Lay Thoughts,' 359
155 'Outspoken Essays,' I. 51
156 'England,' 217
157 'Lay Thoughts,' 215
158 'Lay Thoughts,' 313–314
159 'Lay Thoughts,' 167
160 'Lay Thoughts,' 321–322
161 'England,' 158
162 'Speculum Animae,' 4–5
163 'Outspoken Essays,' II. 207–208
164 'England,' 221
165 'England,' 275
166 'England,' 290
167 'Lay Thoughts,' 147
168 'England,' 269
169 'England,' 268
170 'Lay Thoughts,' 71
171 'Speculum Animae,' 24
172 'Lay Thoughts,' 213
173 'Lay Thoughts,' 50
174 'Lay Thoughts,' 27
175 'Plotinus,' II. 238
176 'Lay Thoughts,' 344
177 'Plotinus,' II. 238
178 'Outspoken Essays,' II. 252
179 'Outspoken Essays,' II. 185
180 'Outspoken Essays,' II. 138
181 'Outspoken Essays,' II. 137–138
182 'Plotinus,' II. 238
183 'Outspoken Essays,' I. 26
184 'Outspoken Essays,' I. 27
185 'Outspoken Essays,' I. 33–34
186 'Lay Thoughts,' 26
187 'Lay Thoughts,' 196
188 'Outspoken Essays,' I. 105
189 'Plotinus,' II. 238–239
190 'Plotinus,' II. 223
191 'Lay Thoughts,' 196
192 'Speculum Animae,' 46
193 'England,' 193

List of References

194 'Lay Thoughts,' 321
195 'Lay Thoughts,' 162
196 'Outspoken Essays,' I. 12
197 'Personal Idealism,' 137
198 'Outspoken Essays,' 159
199 'Lay Thoughts,' 210
200 'Personal Religion,' 66
201 'Outspoken Essays,' I. 32
202 'The Church and the Age,' 67
203 'Lay Thoughts,' 70
204 'Lay Thoughts,' 64
205 'Lay Thoughts,' 66
206 'Lay Thoughts,' 65
207 'Lay Thoughts,' 65
208 'Lay Thoughts,' 23
209 'Lay Thoughts,' 84
210 'Lay Thoughts,' 77
211 'Lay Thoughts,' 75
212 'Lay Thoughts,' 76
213 'Lay Thoughts,' 141–142
214 'Lay Thoughts,' 131–132
215 'Lay Thoughts,' 137
216 'Outspoken Essays,' II. 170
217 'Lay Thoughts,' 138
218 'Lay Thoughts,' 171
219 'Lay Thoughts,' 172
220 'Lay Thoughts,' 177
221 'Lay Thoughts,' 178
222 'Outspoken Essays,' I. 36
223 'Lay Thoughts,' 210
224 'Speculum Animae,' 7
225 'Christian Mysticism,' 24
226 'Speculum Animae,' 8
227 'Outspoken Essays,' II. 25
228 'Personal Idealism,' 111
229 'Outspoken Essays,' I. 9
230 'Lay Thoughts,' 209
231 'Personal Religion,' 72
232 'The Platonic Tradition,' 111
233 'Outspoken Essays,' II. 21–22
234 'Speculum Animae,' 1.
235 'Outspoken Essays,' II. 24
236 'Personal Religion,' 71
237 'Plotinus,' II. 233
238 'Plotinus,' II. 235
239 'Personal Idealism,' 154
240 'Personal Religion,' 77
241 'Personal Religion,' 50
242 'Speculum Animae,' 28